India and UN Peace Operations

Part I

Principles of UN Peacekeeping and Mandate

India and UN Peace Operations

Part I

Principles of UN Peacekeeping and Mandate

Edited by

A K Bardalai and Pradeep Goswami

(Established 1870)

A Joint USI - ICWA Publication

Vij Books India Pvt Ltd
New Delhi (India)

Published by

Vij Books India Pvt Ltd
(Publishers, Distributors & Importers)
2/19, Ansari Road
Delhi – 110 002
Phones: 91-11-43596460, 91-11-47340674
Mob: 98110 94883
e-mail: contact@vijpublishing.com
web : www.vijbooks.in

First Published in India in 2021

Contents

Preface

India's deepening engagement with the United Nations is based on its steadfast commitment to multilateralism and dialogue as the key for achieving shared goals and addressing common challenges faced by the global community. These include those related to peace building and peacekeeping, sustainable development, poverty eradication, environment, climate change, terrorism, disarmament, human rights, health and pandemics, migration, cyber security, space and frontier technologies like Artificial Intelligence, comprehensive reform of the United Nations, including the reform of the Security Council, among others.

India was among the select members of the United Nations that signed the Declaration by United Nations at Washington on 1 January 1942. India also participated in the historic UN Conference of International Organization at San Francisco from 25 April to 26 June 1945. India strongly supports the purposes and principles of the UN and has made significant contributions to implementing the goals of the Charter, and the evolution of the UN's specialized programmes and agencies. India believes that the United Nations and the norms of international relations that it has fostered remain the most efficacious means for tackling today's global challenges. India is steadfast in its efforts to work with the comity of nations in the spirit of multilateralism to achieve comprehensive and equitable solutions to all problems facing us including development and poverty eradication, climate change.

India has a long and distinguished history of service in UN peacekeeping, having contributed more personnel than any other country. To date, more than 253,000 Indians have served in 49 of the 71 UN peacekeeping missions established around the world since 1948. Currently, there are around 5,500 troops & police from India who are deployed to UN peacekeeping missions, the fifth highest amongst troop-contributing countries.

Commencing with its participation in the UN operation in Korea in 1950s, India's mediatory role in resolving the stalemate over prisoners of war in Korea led to the signing of the armistice ending the Korean War. India chaired the five-member Neutral Nations Repatriation Commission while the Indian Custodian Force supervised the process of interviews and repatriation that followed. The UN entrusted Indian armed forces with subsequent peace missions in the Middle East, Cyprus, and the Congo (since 1971, Zaire). India also served as chair of the three international commissions for supervision and control for Vietnam, Cambodia, and Laos established by the 1954 Geneva Accords on Indochina.

India has a long tradition of sending women on UN peacekeeping missions. In 2007, India became the first country to deploy an all-women contingent to a UN peacekeeping mission. Medical care, veterinary support to the domestic animals of the local population and constructional activities are among the many services Indian peacekeepers provide to the communities in which they serve on behalf of the Organization.

India has provided 17 Force Commanders to various missions. Besides the Force Commanders, India also had the honour of providing two Military Advisors, one woman Police Adviser and one Deputy Military Advisor to the Secretary-General of the United Nations. India was the first country to contribute to the Trust Fund on Sexual Exploitation and Abuse, which was set up in 2016. India's longstanding service has not come without cost. 173 Indian peacekeepers have paid the ultimate price while serving with the United Nations. India has lost more peacekeepers than any other member state.

In the more than seven decades of UN peacekeeping operations' interventions in different kinds of conflict, peacekeepers always faced multiple challenges when it comes to implementing the mandate. As time passes, these challenges have become more complex undermining the ability of the peace operations to deliver in the conflict zone. This is also what the Department of UN Peace Operation's survey of August 2019 indicates. Besides the inherent lag between the intent and the outcome in all spheres of the activities, there could be several other strategic and operational reasons for slow progress in reform in the field. This is not to conclude that so far, no reform has taken place. India has been one of the oldest contributors in peacekeeping operations and hence is a vast repository of the best practices. The United Service Institution (USI) of India in the past has taken the lead in providing the platform for organising discourse and research in the field of UN peace operations to put across an Indian perspective on a few most crucial attributes of the current challenges that face reform of the UN peace operations. At this juncture, United Service Institution of India (USI) (https://usiofindia.org), the oldest think tank in India, in collaboration with Indian Council of World Affairs (ICWA) (https://www.icwa.in) the premium think tank of India's Ministry of External Affairs, Government of India, planned to conduct a series of Webinars on UN peace operations in 2021 on the following themes:

- ➢ Theme 1 - India and UN Peace Operations: Principles of UN Peacekeeping and Mandate

- ➢ Theme 2 - UN Peace Operations: Hostage-taking of Peacekeepers.

- ➢ Theme 3 - Protection of civilians in complex UN Peace Operations.

- ➢ Theme 4 - Why UN peacekeeping succeeds or fails?

- ➢ Theme 5 - Peacekeeping reform: An Indian perspective.

- ➢ Theme 6 - Interoperability Challenges in multidimensional peace operations: role of senior mission leaders (Head of the Mission and Force Commanders)

- ➢ Theme 7 - Peace and Security: the role of women.

The first in the series of USI – ICWA: UN Webinars, was conducted on 27 Feb 2021 on "India and UN Peace Operations: Principles of UN Peacekeeping and Mandate" with the following sub-themes:

- ➢ Principles of UN Peacekeeping, its continued relevance and mandate implementation.

- ➢ Relevance of the principle of "Use of Force" in MONUSCO and UNMISS.

- ➢ Contribution of traditional UN peace operations (UNIFIL and UNDOF) for sustainable peace.

This monograph is a compilation of talks by eminent speakers during the webinar.

About the Participants

Major General BK Sharma, AVSM, SM (Retd)** is the Director of the USI of India (USI), India's oldest think tank established by the British in 1870. He has tenanted prestigious assignments in India, including command of a mountain division on China border and Senior Faculty Member at the National Defence College. He has represented his country at the UN as Military Observer in Central America and has been India's Defence Attaché in Central Asia. He specializes in Strategic Net Assessment methodology, Scenario Building and Strategic Gaming.

Dr TCA Raghavan, a former officer of the Indian Foreign Service, was the Indian High Commissioner to Pakistan (2013-15) and currently is the Director-General of ICWA. He had earlier served as Deputy High Commissioner in Pakistan (2003-2007) and High Commissioner to Singapore from 2009 to 2013. He has also served in Kuwait, the United Kingdom, and Bhutan. His first book was published in January 2020: "*Attendant Lords, Bairam Khan and Abdur Rahim - Courtiers and Poets in Mughal India*". His latest book was published recently and is entitled "*The People Next Door - The curious history of India's relations with Pakistan*".

Lieutenant General Satish Nambiar, PVSM, AVSM, VrC (Retd) a veteran of the 1965 and 1971 wars, a graduate of the Australian Staff College, he has served the Indian Army within India and abroad and is a former Director of The USI of India. He was the first Force Commander and Head of Mission of the United Nations forces in the former

Yugoslavia (UNPROFOR). During his tenure as the Director of USI, he was appointed as Adviser to the Government of Sri Lanka on the peace process in that country from 2002 to 2003 and was the member of the UN 16-member high-level panel to study global security threats and recommend measures for effective collective action. The General is the recipient of the Indian national award of Padma Bhushan for his contribution to National Security Affairs.

Shri Asoke Mukerji, IFS (Retd), a former officer of Indian Foreign Service who has served in the United States, the United Kingdom, the Russian Federation, Kazakhstan, United Arab Emirates, Geneva, Soviet Central Asia and the former Yugoslavia. He was also India's Ambassador and Permanent Representative to the United Nations in 2015. He has been Special Secretary in the Ministry of External Affairs responsible for International Organizations as well as India's Foreign Policy Planning and Review and was awarded a Doctor of Civil Laws (honoris causa) degree by the University of East Anglia in the UK for his contributions to diplomacy in July 2018. He has been an elected member of the Governing Council of India's oldest think-tank, the United Service Institution, and a Distinguished Fellow of the Vivekananda International Foundation. He authored a book *"India and the United Nations: a Photo Journey 1945-2015"* in September 2015.

Dr Cedric de Coning (South Africa) is a Research Professor with the Norwegian Institute of International Affairs (NUPI), where he also co-convenes the NUPI Centre on UN and Global Governance and coordinates the Effectiveness of Peace Operations Network (EPON). He is also a Senior Advisor for the African Centre for the Constructive Resolution of Disputes (ACCORD). He holds a PhD in Applied Ethics from the Department of Philosophy at the University of Stellenbosch in South Africa. His research covers African and United Nations peace and security issues. He has served in a number of advisory capacities for the African Union and United Nations, including on the UN Secretary-General's Advisory Board for the Peacebuilding Fund and co-edited several books.

Lieutenant General Chander Prakash, SM, VSM (Retd) is a veteran of Indian Army and has held a number of important military command and staff appointments at various levels both in India and abroad. He was Indian Defence Advisor in France from 2005 to 2008, the Senior Sector Operations Officer in United Nations Iran-Iraq Military Observers Group, on the Board of Management at Centre for UN Peacekeeping (CUNPK), New Delhi and later Force Commander of UN Peacekeeping Mission in the Democratic Republic of Congo (MONUSCO) from August 2010 to March 2013. Post retirement from active service of the army, he served as the Deputy Director and Editor at USI of India, New Delhi.

Lieutenant General IS Singha, AVSM, VSM (Retd) is a veteran of Indian Army and has held a number of important military command and staff appointments at various levels both in India and abroad. He was the Chief Logistics Officer in the United Nations Mission in Ethiopia and Eretria and subsequently the Force Commander and Head of Mission of the United Nations Disengagement Force at Golan Heights (UNDOF). After retirement, General is presently the Director of Global and Government Affairs at TAC Security, a leading global cyber security company which is working in partnership with USI of India.

Lieutenant General JP Nehra, PVSM, AVSM (Retd) with a rich operational, administrative, and academic experience, held a variety of coveted assignments in India and abroad. He was Inspector-General Assam Rifles looking after the troubled state of Nagaland in 2008-09. Subsequently, he commanded one of the largest operational corps in Jammu & Kashmir, responsible for Line of Control as also Counter-Terrorist operations. He was the Deputy Force Commander and Deputy Head of Mission of the United Nations Mission in Lebanon (UNIFIL) in 2006-2008. He has held the appointment of the Adjutant General of the Indian Army in 2011 and served as the Deputy Chief of Army Staff until his retirement in Oct 2014. He is currently working as the Principal Advisor, Confederation of Indian Industry (CII).

Major General AK Bardalai (Retd) has held various command and staff assignments at different levels including the command of an infantry division. He was also the Commandant of the Indian Military Training Team in Bhutan from October 2011 to January 2014. Earlier, he served as a Military Observer in the United Nations Verification Mission in Angola in 1991-92 and was the Deputy Head of the Mission and Deputy Force Commander of United Nations Interim Forces in Lebanon (UNIFIL) from 2008 to 2010.

Major General PK Goswami, VSM (Retd) is Deputy Director at the USI of India, New Delhi and chief coordinator for series of USI – ICWA Webinars on UN peace operations. He was Military Observer with United Nations Verification Mission at Angola (UNAVEM) in 1991-92 and Senior Faculty at National Defence College, New Delhi. He represented National Defence College, India at 16th ASEAN Regional Forum for Heads of Defence Universities, Colleges and Institutions at Beijing, China in Nov 2012.

Major General SB Asthana, SM, VSM (Retd) is an Indian Army Veteran. He held important assignments during his service career and served in UNMEE as the Logistic Officer. Post retirement, in addition to pursuing his academic studies, he is on board of several strategic think tanks across the world. He is a prolific writer and erudite speaker on security matters. He is currently the Chief Instructor of military courses at USI of India.

Opening Remarks

*Major General BK Sharma, AVSM, SM** (Retd)*

India's role and participation in the UN peacekeeping operations (UNPKO) is well known and internationally appreciated. The USI has played a stellar role in the furtherance of India's UNPKO endeavours. The Centre for United Nations Peace Keeping (CUNPK) was established at the USI under the visionary leadership of Gen Nambiar. The CUNPK was nurtured by the USI for 14 long years to become a regional Centre for excellence in the UNPK capacity building and practicing UN diplomacy. The CUNPK has now grown to become a full-fledged unit of the Indian Army.

USI is also a member of the Challenges Forum and EPON (Effectiveness of Peacekeeping Network). Our UN experts have interacted with HIPPO Panel (High Level Independent Panel of Peace Operations) and participated in the UN events in the framework of R2P, under the aegis of MEA. We have regularly hosted and participated in UNPK international conferences and workshops. The USI has conducted a series of courses for international participants in collaboration with UNITAR (United National Institution for Training and Research). USI, in past, had organized lectures by high-ranking UN dignitaries, including Mr Kofi Annan, who was then the UN Secretary General and also conducted international programmes on protection of women in the conflict zones.

The USI has published books and monographs on the UNPKO. Our Institution is endowed with a highly experienced resource faculty, comprising Indian permanent representatives to the UN, Heads of UN peacekeeping missions, those who have tenanted staff and advisory appointments at the UN HQ at the policy-making level, besides a vast reservoir of UN Military Observers from military, paramilitary and police forces.

Since inception of PKO in 1948 world over 71 PKO have been undertaken. Presently, there are 14 missions with more than 85,000 uniformed personnel deployed across the world. India is actively participating in several sensitive UNPK missions.

UNPKO is an onerous mandate, and the principles of peacekeeping are rooted in the lofty ideals of human dignity comprehensive humanitarian security. UNPK in its evolutionary journey has a mix bag of hits and misses. It goes without saying that with the passage of time, the planning and conduct of UNPKO has become more complex and daunting. Nature of conflicts has morphed from the classic inter-state to intra-state conflicts with non-state actors and state proxies playing a major role. Besides, there are other more complex trans-border non-traditional security threats such as pandemics, calamities, organised crime, cyber security, and the like. And today we are in the era of overly complex grey zone conflicts.

PM Narendra Modi in his speech at the 75th UN Gen Assembly session, on "the future we want, the UN we need" had alluded to a commonly held belief that the UN is presently facing a crisis of command and he had made a strong pitch for UN reforms and restructuring with a view to develop a deeper sense of multi-literalism for conflict resolution and mitigation of non-traditional security threats.

It is in the light of aforesaid, the USI and ICWA planned to hold a series of webinars for the cross-fertilization of ideas and for generating policy recommendations for reforms and restructuring of the UN, particularly the UNPKO. This initiative assumes added importance at a juncture when India is a member of the UN Security Council.

I am sanguine that today's event will prove to be critical curtain raiser for our further engagement and dialogue on this hugely important subject of international importance.

Keynote Address

Lieutenant General Satish Nambiar, PVSM, AVSM, VrC (Retd)

Background

As one of the founding members of the United Nations, India's contribution to the maintenance of international peace and security has been second to none. In no other field of activity has this been manifested more than in United Nations peace operations commencing with our participation in the operations in Korea in 1950. Over the years, India provided commanders, military observers, staff officers, contingents, and in later years civilian police, to many of the United Nations missions deployed to keep the peace in various parts of the world. The use of armed military contingents was first authorised by the United Nations Security Council (UNSC) for deployment with the United Nations Emergency Force in the Gaza Strip and the Sinai after the Arab-Israeli war in 1956. From 15 November 1956 to 19 May 1967, eleven infantry battalions from India successively served with this force, total of over 13000 all ranks. The initial success of this force led the Security Council to readily accept a request by the Congo in 1960 for intervention on attaining independence from Belgium; for which India provided two successive brigade groups during the period 1960-64. Since then, Indian contingents have been part of UN peacekeeping operations in Cyprus, Namibia, Cambodia, Mozambique,

Somalia, Angola, Liberia, Rwanda, Congo, Sudan/South Sudan, Lebanon, the Golan Heights, Sierra Leone, Ethiopia/Eritrea, and so on. As it happens, India has participated in every peacekeeping operation in Africa, except the current one in Mali.

India has a somewhat unique and enviable record in terms of the contribution for training of UN peacekeepers today. A Centre for United Nations Peacekeeping (CUNPK) was established under the United Service Institution of India in September 2000 at Delhi, with support from the Ministries of External Affairs and Defence, and Army Headquarters. Since then, this Centre besides overseeing the training of contingents earmarked for peacekeeping operations, undertakes/conducts training courses for our sub-unit commanders, military observers, and officers earmarked for deputation on staff appointments. It is a measure of our commitment to the UN, that a minimum of fifteen vacancies on each of the international courses that are conducted (about twice a year), are offered to developing countries; with all expenses incurred on travel from home country and back, training, accommodation and meals, borne by the Ministry of External Affairs, Government of India. A number of developed countries like the USA, UK, Australia, Japan, Norway, Singapore, etc also subscribe to these courses on a self-financing arrangement. It is indeed a matter of great satisfaction and pride that, in the last twenty years, the CUNPK has established itself internationally as a Centre of Excellence, and is now often called upon to conduct specialised international courses on behalf of UN DPKO, as also joint initiatives with other countries and with international organisations like the International Committee of the Red Cross (ICRC).

Dilemmas and Challenges of UN Peacekeeping Today

In preparing ourselves for continued participation in United Nations peacekeeping operations into the 21st Century, we must take into account the radical changes in the nature of the peacekeeping commitment. United Nations peacekeepers are increasingly being sent to regions where civil-war type situations prevail; where there are no agreements, or if there are, these are rather tenuous, or broken without compunction; where the consent or cooperation of the belligerent parties cannot be relied upon; where constitutional authority does not exist in many cases, or if it does, there is limited control. In such situations, today's peacekeepers are not only required to keep the warring parties apart to the extent they can, but are increasingly called upon to undertake peace-building operations; safeguard humanitarian relief operations, monitor human rights violations, assist in mine clearance, monitor state boundaries or borders, provide civilian police support, assist in rebuilding logistics infra-structure like roads, railways, bridges, and to support electoral processes.

Protection of civilians has become a mandated task for almost all UN peacekeeping missions deployed these days; a task with many ramifications that need to be understood by the political and military leadership. There is a great deal that can be stated on the subject, but for the purpose of this paper, a few important points are made. Use of force for protection and implementation of the mission mandate was first resorted to in United Nations Operation in The Congo (ONUC) in the early 1960s. As mentioned earlier, India had two successive brigade groups in that mission and this was used to launch combat operations against mercenaries and Katangese rebels led by Moise Tshombe. In the process, the Indian contingent suffered a number of fatalities (36) and many more injured (124). Hence, this is not a new concept or phenomenon. But it needs to be carefully calibrated and located within a credible political framework both locally and internationally. This invariably poses problems because of inadequate political support to missions that are set up. Regional players, as also the major powers, pursue their own agenda that in many cases do not necessarily complement the mission mandate.

The use of force demands that appropriate resources be made available. In almost all UN missions deployed today, this is wanting because those who have the resources both in terms of trained manpower and equipment, (namely, the developed world), are not participating in UN peacekeeping operations. If UN peacekeeping is to remain effective, the developed world must return to the commitment. And this should go beyond the present arrangement of seeking positions in senior management and command, to provision of "boots on the ground". The connotations of the use of force must be clearly understood by Security Council members who mandate it, the staff at UN HQ, and by troop contributors; and the concept imaginatively evolved. Peacekeepers must be mentally and physically attuned to the fact that the use of force will mean inflicting casualties on belligerents, and, that casualties may well be incurred by members of the force.

Following up on the views expressed above, I am of the view that there is an imperative need for troop contributor countries like India to deliberate, analyse and address the following three issues in context of the calls being made for deployment of UN peacekeepers:

➢ To deal with terrorism.

➢ To prosecute operations under the Responsibility to Protect (R2P) regime.

➢ Peacebuilding being mandated as a task for UN peacekeepers.

Deployment of UN Peacekeepers to Deal with Terrorism

On the issue of use of UN peacekeepers to deal with terrorism, there would be no disagreement with the postulation that dealing with terrorists attacking UN peacekeepers deployed in a mission area is one thing, and the Security Council mandating the deployment of a UN peacekeeping force to deal with terrorism in a member state is an entirely different issue. To buttress my argument about dealing with the former situation, permit me to reflect on something I was personally involved in as an example of what our approach should be. A few months after my return to the rolls of the Indian Army in March 1993 having declined an offer of extension in the assignment as the Head of Mission and Force Commander of the UN mission in the former Yugoslavia (UNPROFOR), the Government of India and Army Headquarters were grappling with the task of putting together a brigade group sized force for deployment to Somalia as part of a UN Security Council mandated peacekeeping mission following the withdrawal of the US led forces that had been deployed there without achieving the intended results.

General Bipin Joshi who had by then taken over as the Chief of the Army Staff (and incidentally had experience as a young staff officer in the rank of captain in United Nations Emergency Force in the Gaza Strip and the Sinai in the early 1960s) asked for any suggestions in context of my recent experiences. The only recommendation that I shall relate in context of the current discussions, is the one I made about the equipping the contingent. In context of my personal experience in UNPROFOR (where I incidentally did not have any Indian personnel under my command other than one staff officer), I advised the Chief that while we may take note of the list of items of equipment the contingent was expected to take with it, and for which the UN HQ would reimburse costs, we should ensure the contingent was equipped with enough 'muscular' capacity to deal with anyone who dared challenge its authority. As a consequence, the contingent went in not only with its normal complement of personal and support weapons and ammunition, but with a troop of tanks, a battery of heavy mortars, and a couple of attack helicopters. In the event, their presence certainly conveyed a message to the local fighters. A bunch of renegade fighters who tried to take on a patrol was given such a lesson that no further attempts were made. As it transpired, the tank troop did not have to fire a single round of tank ammunition, nor did the heavy mortar battery go into action; but their very presence and the message conveyed that they would be used if required, was deterrent enough.

The attack helicopters came in handy ironically in a situation that called for providing assistance in extricating elements of the Pakistani contingent that was under attack. Hence there is no question that should "spoilers", "renegades", "terrorist groups", etc engage our troops in the course of execution of mission tasks, they must be dealt with as in combat situations; given an option to surrender—or eliminated. Needless to say, this also calls for support to the troops and contingents from the top military and political leadership against the ubiquitous human rights activists.

My reservation on the subject is about calls at various forums in recent times for the UN Security Council to mandate deployment of UN peacekeepers to deal with terrorists operating within member states. In my view, should there be a need for the UN to deal with such contingencies the Security Council should mandate a Chapter VII enforcement operation under a regional organisation or a lead country; in which case, combat operations using all means at the disposal of member states should be launched against the organisation or group. The problem really is, the powers that have the clout in the international arena including the UN (namely the developed countries that have the trained manpower and state-of-the-art equipment resources), invariably try to avoid having their hands tainted by participating in such interventions, and hence try and palm these off to the developing countries to handle under the convenient façade of UN peacekeeping. It is time that countries like India call this bluff.

Deployment of UN peacekeepers under the 'Responsibility to Protect' (R2P) Regime

There is an increasing tendency within sections of the international community to try and cloak some interventions, and possibly UN peacekeeping missions, under the R2P regime. As someone who was a member of Kofi Annan's High-Level Panel that recommended the adoption of the concept in the 2005 World Summit, my personal view is quite unambiguous - R2P is not for UN peacekeeping. If there are situations of genocide, war crimes, ethnic cleansing and crimes against humanity that the international community determines merits action, it is for the Security Council to mandate intervention in terms of Chapter VII of the UN Charter by military forces under the aegis of a regional organisation or under a lead nation. It is not only hypocritical but positively unacceptable, that the powerful countries that run things at the UN try and avoid this responsibility by dumping it (as for dealing with terrorism) on the developing world, again under the façade of UN peacekeeping.

And, in rounding off this observation, permit me to quote an extract from a book written by a fellow member on the High Level Panel, and former Foreign Minister of Australia, Gareth Evans—'The Responsibility to Protect, Ending Mass Atrocity Crimes Once and for All'—the Brookings Institution 2008. Evans states that "the divide between the Western world and the developing countries is somewhat starkly and possibly ironically highlighted by the fact that three major instances where R2P intervention could plausibly have been justified on strong humanitarian grounds, since they protect people seriously at risk from the actions of their own governments, were categorised as intrusions on sovereignty. The first instance was India's action in December 1971 in East Pakistan where large scale genocide and displacement was occasioned by the brutal suppression of the local population by the national authorities. The second case was Cambodia where Vietnam's actions brought to a halt the atrocities inflicted on the population from 1975 to 1978 by the Khmer Rouge. The third case was Tanzania's overthrow in 1979 of the murderous Idi Amin regime in Uganda. One cannot but cynically conclude that the Western world labelled these instances as aggression because the actions were initiated by developing countries."

Peace-building being Mandated as a Task for UN Peacekeepers

The decision to make 'peace-building' part of the mandate of UN peacekeepers is a retrograde step on which I have reservations, because whereas there is little doubt that military personnel are more than capable of undertaking peace-building activities when required and have done so to great effect on many occasions, it is not a task they should be additionally burdened with.

Firstly, because they are not trained for it; and secondly, the fact that they move out of the mission area on completion of tenures of six months or a year make them unsuitable for tasks that require sustained effort over a prolonged period. In my view, it is a task for other UN agencies organised for the purpose, and international/regional governmental and non-governmental organisations that have been set up, funded, and mandated, for just that sort of work. It was therefore with good reason that in defining the elements of peace operations, the Brahimi Panel Report clearly enunciated that "United Nations peace operations entail three principal activities: one conflict prevention and peace-making; two peace-keeping; and three peace-building." And went on to state that, "Long term conflict prevention addresses the structural sources of conflict in order to build a solid foundation for peace. Where those foundations are crumbling, conflict prevention attempts to reinforce them, usually in the form of a diplomatic initiative. Such preventive action is, by definition, a low-profile activity; when successful, it may even go unnoticed altogether".

Peace-making addresses conflicts in progress and attempting to bring them to a halt, using the tools of diplomacy and mediation. Peacemakers may be envoys of Governments, groups of States, regional organizations, or the United Nations, or they may be unofficial and non-governmental groups, as was the case, for example, in the negotiations leading up to a peace accord for Mozambique. Peace-making may even be the work of a prominent personality, working independently.

Peacekeeping is a 50-year-old enterprise that has evolved rapidly in the past decade from a traditional, primarily military model of observing ceasefires and force separations after inter-State wars, to incorporate a complex model of many elements, military and civilian, working together to maintain peace in the dangerous aftermath of civil wars.

Peace-building is a term of more recent origin that, as used in the 'present report', defines activities undertaken on the far side of the conflict to reassemble the foundations of peace and provide the tools for building on those foundations, something that is more than just the absence of war. Thus, peace-building includes but is not limited to reintegrating former combatants into civilian society, strengthening the rule of law (for example, through training and restructuring of local police, and judicial and penal reform); improving respect for human rights through the monitoring, education and investigation of past and existing abuses; providing technical assistance for democratic development (including electoral assistance and support for free media); and promoting conflict resolution and reconciliation techniques."

Principles of UN Peacekeeping

Shri Asoke Mukerji, IFS (Retd)

Background

The UN Charter does not provide any principles of UN Peacekeeping. In 1948, when the ceasefire was arranged between Egypt and Israel after their first war, the UN Security Council (UNSC) mandated the deployment of unarmed troops from UN member states that volunteered to send such troops. The first UN peacekeeping mission (PKO) called UN Truce Supervision Organization (UNSTO) was composed of 148 military observers contributed by Western European countries, Australia, and New Zealand to monitor the Egypt-Israel ceasefire, so that political efforts to resolve the crisis could be implemented.

The second PKO deployed by the UNSC is of course familiar to us in India. This is the UN Military Observer Group for India and Pakistan (UNMOGIP), which deployed in January 1949 and became a mandated operation after the India-Pakistan Karachi Agreement of July 1949. Following the 1971 India-Pakistan War and the July 1972 Shimla Agreement Treaty formalising the terms for concluding the war, there is no role for the UNMOGIP for India-Pakistan conflicts today, as it does not feature in the Shimla Agreement. UNMOGIP continues to be funded not from the UN peacekeeping budget, but from the UN's regular budget. For some time now, there have been calls to wind up

PKOs which drain the regular budget of the UN, including UNMOGIP. This call was repeated most recently by India's Ambassador to the United Nations. However, the politics of PKOs played by the UNSC's five permanent members (P5) who take decisions for the Council has delayed the implementation of this call so far.

India's participation in the initial UNPKOs, beginning with the deployment of Indian UN troops in the Korean War (1950), resulted in a growing pool of Indian military officers seconded to the UN whose professionalism and experience have contributed to UN peacekeeping doctrine.

In 1950, soon after India's independence, the first Indian troops to be deployed under the UN flag were from the 60 Parachute Field Ambulance of the Indian Army. This unit was sent to provide medical cover to US/ROK and UN forces engaged in the Korean War. The unit served in Korea for a total of three and a half years (November 1950 - May 1954), the longest single tenure by any military unit under the UN flag.

Between 1948 and 1956, the UN Security Council did not authorize armed troops for peacekeeping missions. It was only during the Suez Canal Crisis in 1956, when the United Kingdom and France invaded Egypt, that the first armed troops contributed by UN member states were deployed in a more robust manner to keep the peace.

As General Satish Nambiar, a former Director of USI, has written in his magisterial review of India's UN PKOs, between 15 November 1956 to 19 May 1967, eleven infantry battalions from India served by rotation in the UN Emergency Force (UNEF 1) to ensure the withdrawal of France, U.K., and Israel from Egyptian territory and to sustain the peace between Israel and her Arab neighbours. 27 Indian UN peacekeepers lost their lives in this operation.

In 1960, the Congo requested for deployment of UN peacekeepers to counter secession and re-integrate the country after Belgian rule. Between 14 July 1960 and 30 June 1964, two Indian brigades participated in ONUC UNPKO. This is a good example to counter uninformed criticism of PKOs for being unable to use force to defend their mandate. The rules of engagement of ONUC were modified to cater for use of force in defence of the mandate, in carrying out humanitarian tasks, and in countering mercenaries. 39 Indian personnel lost their lives in the operation. Captain Gurbachan Singh Salaria became the only Indian UN peacekeeper to receive the Param Vir Chakra, India's highest military award, for laying down his life in defence of the UN mandate in the Congo.

Principles of Peacekeeping

These early experiences of India's UN peacekeepers were the raw data for developing the principles of UN peacekeeping today. The contribution of Major General I J Rikhye, appointed as the first Military Adviser to the UN Secretary-General between 1960-1967, was seminal in this context. Three core principles of effective UN peacekeeping were identified based on the experience of UNPKOs on the ground. These are:

1. Deployment with the consent of the parties,

2. Impartiality in operations, and

3. Non-use of force except in self-defence and defence of the mandate.

Subsequent contributions to UN peacekeeping doctrine by Indian military officers have built on this, both at UN Headquarters (where two Indian Generals have served as Military Advisers in recent years) and in the field (where almost a score of Indian Generals have acted as Force Commanders with distinction).

Application of Principles of Peacekeeping

Three broad areas have evolved in UN peacekeeping where the application of these fundamental UN peacekeeping principles is being tested.

1. **Political Transition to Peace.** The first area is in making use of UN peacekeeping across the world to ensure a political transition to peace. Such UNPKOs include UNPROFOR in the former Yugoslavia, whose first Force Commander was India's General Satish Nambiar; UNTAC in Cambodia; ONUSAL in El Salvador; ONUMOZ in Mozambique; UNOSOM in Somalia; UNAVEM in Angola; UNAMSIL in Sierra Leone; UNMEE in Ethiopia-Eritrea; UNMIT in East Timor and of course UNMISS in South Sudan, which today has unfortunately become a tragic victim of the ineffectiveness of the UN Security Council to perform its mandated responsibilities.

2. **Peacebuilding Activities.** The second area is in augmenting peacebuilding activities by encouraging and mentoring the strengthening of national governance institutions. UNTAG saw Indian peacekeepers assist in the creation of the institutions of an independent Namibia. India became the first country to demonstrate the effectiveness of women as UN peacekeepers in peacebuilding with the deployment of the first all-female formed police unit (FFPU) to the UNPKO in Liberia (UNMIL) in 2007. When UNMIL was wound up in February 2018, President Sirleaf of Liberia commented: "The contribution you have made in inspiring Liberian women, imparting in them the spirit of

professionalism and encouraging them to join operations that protect the nation, for that we will always be grateful."

3. **Response to New Challenges.** The third area is in leading the ground level response to new challenges. India's experience has shown that a professional approach to implementing the principles of peacekeeping to uphold impartiality in peacekeeping can pay dividends.

4. The end of the Cold War resulted in a mushrooming of crises. More than 20 new UNPKOs were deployed between 1989-1994 alone. India's contributions to these new operations rose significantly. However, the challenges posed by the ground situation altered dramatically, with the focus on operating in a civil war situation where protection of civilians caught in the violence became the mandate of the PKO.

Priorities for Application of Principles of Peacekeeping

The three priorities for applying the principles of UN PKOs are—an effective implementation of the core mandate to protect civilians caught in conflicts, countering the increasing acts of terrorism directed against PKOs like MINUSMA, and reviving the reason for which PKOs were conceptualized, i.e. reaching a political solution to the conflict.

Protection of Civilians

The most important challenge faced by UNPKO principles on the ground today relates to the protection of civilians caught in intra-state conflicts. In theory, many UN member-states in the UN General Assembly have pledged to focus on this issue through the Kigali Principles.

On the ground, protection of civilians is an area where India's UN peacekeepers have made a positive difference, especially in complex UNPKOs like MONUSCO in the Democratic Republic of Congo and UNMISS in South Sudan. In both these PKOs, on which there will be a detailed discussion just after this presentation, the challenges to UN peacekeeping principles are obvious.

In MONUSCO, since 2013 there has been an attempt to make UN peacekeeping troops act in a robust and "interventionist" manner to assist the government of the DRC to neutralize anti-government militias, represented by the M-23 in the Kivu District bordering Rwanda and Uganda. The news earlier this week of the continued activities of militia groups in this volatile region of the DRC, which resulted in the killing of the Italian Ambassador to the DRC and an Italian military policeman while travelling in a MONUSCO escorted convoy, illustrates that there are limitations on the ground to the ability of "robust intervention" by UN peacekeepers to bring about sustainable peace and security.

In UNMISS, the problem is even more ironic. The UN deployed its PKO to assist the newly independent country of South Sudan to transition to its socio-economic development in July 2012. Today, the government of South Sudan openly characterises UNMISS as working against the government in the country. This is even though, going beyond the call of duty, UN peacekeepers have volunteered medical services, including veterinary support, and engineering services, in these UNPKOs, which has contributed to sustaining the livelihood of conflict-impacted local communities.

At the same time, the fact that the core mandate given by the UN Security Council to 11 out of the 13 active PKOs today is to protect civilians caught in the conflict gives the UN peacekeeper potentially an interventionist role, taking over the normal governance tasks of the host country. By their very nature, intra-state disputes require a different approach for successful preventive diplomacy. There are three issues, which are of critical importance for the success of such UN PKOs:

> The most important requirement is the availability of direct inputs from the ground to the Security Council about the triggers of the dispute on its agenda, while respecting the sovereignty of concerned member states.

> A pro-active role must be played by the Security Council for an "inclusive" negotiated peaceful solution, involving all legitimate parties.

> The right people and resources must be deployed by the Security Council on the ground if the UN is to sustain the eventual peace solution.

The unsustainability of using armed force to achieve what preventive diplomacy, including preventive deployment and mediation, are meant to achieve has adversely impacted on both the effectiveness and deployment of UN peacekeeping missions. The Security Council's abdication of a predominant political approach to conflicts on its agenda where it has deployed UN peacekeepers has effectively made UN peacekeepers party to the conflict, rather than facilitators of preventive diplomacy. More significantly, the mandate to use armed force glossed over collateral operational or legal implications, both of which impact adversely on the objective of preventive diplomacy.

The Council is regularly updated with information about the political, security, and socio-economic situation on the ground. It has information about the belligerents or disputants. It controls the flow of human, financial, and technical resources for the UN personnel on the ground. Yet it fails to prevent the spiralling violence on the ground and loses credibility.

Countering Terrorist Threats to PKOs

UN peacekeeping principles face another growing challenge for which they do not have a solution. These are terrorist threats to the UN by non-state actors. Whether it was UNDOF in 2013 due to the emergence of the Syrian conflict, or it is MINUSMA today where the fragmentation of the political landscape in Mali continues to be ignored, it is a fact that most UN peacekeepers who have laid down their lives on duty today have been casualties of terrorist acts. The bulk of the 231 UN peacekeepers who have died on duty in MINUSMA belong to this category.

The Security Council continues its ostrich-like approach to the robust countering of terrorism directed against UN peacekeepers, despite targeted enforcement measures like sanctions and armed force leading to prosecution being available to the Council under Chapter VII of the UN Charter when it deploys UN PKOs.

The Primacy of a Political Solution

At a Leaders' Summit on Peace Operations, held in New York in September 2015, world leaders including India's Prime Minister Shri Narendra Modi deliberated on how UN peacekeeping principles could be made more effective to make the UN more effective on the ground to facilitate the primacy of political solutions to conflicts.

Apart from making the use of PKO resources (human, equipment and financial) more cost-effective, which would include skilling and upgrading of PKOs, the main lesson learnt from successful PKOs is the need to have a finite mandate, i.e. an outer time limit agreed to by the parties to the conflict within which PKOs will help create conditions for a sustainable political settlement.

This was the wisdom brought into the High-Level Independent Panel on Peace Operations (HIPPO) by its Chairman, former President and Nobel Laureate Ramos Horta. The Report of the HIPPO circulated as both a UN General Assembly and a UNSC document in fact provides interested parties with a blueprint on the way forward. Subsequently, the UN Secretary-General has initiated an "Action for Peacekeeping (A4P)" framework as a renewal of political support for UN PKOs that is endorsed by over 150 member-states of the UN General Assembly, including India.

The Way Forward

However, to achieve effective UN PKOs on the ground, the action lies with the UNSC which is the body mandating these operations, including their principles. Due to well-known constraints including polarization among the P5, the UNSC has been inactive so far. However, two linked options suggest themselves as the way forward to make UN peacekeeping principles relevant on the ground.

One is an immediate, short-term option. Article 44 of the UN Charter provides for the Council to get direct inputs regarding the political and security situation from the ground, which would help it to tailor its mandates, from the troop contributing countries of its peacekeeping operations who are not represented in the Council. However, because of the adamant refusal of its permanent members to invite troop contributing countries which are not members of the Council, into its deliberations on this issue, the Council has chosen to completely ignore this direct input while considering the actual situation on the ground. Getting experienced troop contributing countries actively involved in decisions of the Security Council to make the deployment of

UN peacekeepers more effective is a logical way, for example, to get regional perspectives by troop-contributing countries as well as elected members from regional groups into Security Council decision-making, especially for PKOs Africa which face the brunt of the challenges to UN peacekeeping today.

The second way is long-term and structural, focused on reforming the body that implements the principles of UN peacekeeping, which is the Security Council. World leaders gave a unanimous mandate fifteen years ago for "early reform" of the UNSC "to make it more broadly representative, efficient and transparent and thus to further enhance its effectiveness and the legitimacy and implementation of its decisions". This rationale for UNSC reform is even more valid in 2021, as the P5 use their veto privilege to prevent the UNSC from resolving major crises confronting the world.

When India's Prime Minister Shri Narendra Modi proposed that the UN commemorate the fallen UN peacekeepers by constructing a Memorial Wall, the number of troops under the UN flag that had laid down their lives in defence of the principles of the UN Charter was about 3300. That number has increased dramatically to over 4000 today. Until the UN undertakes these steps, the troops deployed on UN PKOs will continue to face serious challenges to their effective functioning. Unfortunately, the human cost of delay in UN reforms is mounting daily, including for UN peacekeepers.

Relevance of the Principles of Use of Force: The Case of UNMISS

Dr Cedric de Coning

Abstract

The UN Mission in South Sudan (UNMISS) provides us with two key challenges when it comes to the use of force in the context of the Protection of Civilians (POC) mandate. Firstly, it raises the question of whether it is realistic for a UN peacekeeping mission to use force against host nation forces. Secondly, it presents an ethical dilemma, namely whether peacekeepers need to prioritize protecting the few over the many.

Background: From Independence to Civil War

The independence of South Sudan was the culmination of 6-year process which began with the Comprehensive Peace Agreement (CPA) of 2005. The UN oversaw the implementation of the CPA and organized a referendum in January 2011 to determine the status of Southern Sudan.

The UN Mission in South Sudan (UNMISS) took over from the UN Mission in Sudan (UNMIS) on 8 July 2011, the day before South Sudan's independence. On 15 December 2013, violence broke out between two factions of the Sudan People's Liberation Movement (SPLM), which quickly spread across most of the rest of the country. A peace agreement, the Agreement on the Resolution of the Conflict in the Republic of South (ARCSS), was signed in August 2015 and lasted for almost a year before it violently broke down in July 2016. The war raged on for a further three years before a new peace agreement was reached in September 2019, the Revitalized Agreement on the Resolution of the Conflict in the Republic of South Sudan (R-ARCSS).

When the civil war started in December 2013, the Government of South Sudan suspected UNMISS of supporting the opposition forces and although the relationship has improved since then, it remains challenging. A study into the effectiveness of UNMISS undertaken by the Effectiveness of Peace Operations Network (EPON) in 2019 found that obstructions to the freedom of movement of the mission by the Government and other actors was a major factor impeding the performance of the mission. An independent review commissioned by the Security Council late in 2020 similarly found that such obstructions were "the single most important factor limiting the Mission's ability to carry out its mandated activities."

The outbreak of the civil war in 2013 triggered one of the largest humanitarian crises in the world. Hundreds of thousands of people died in the conflict and thousands more fled the violence. As of March 2021, more than 1.6 million South Sudanese remain internally displaced and approximately 2.2 million South Sudanese has sought refuge in neighbouring countries and beyond.

When the civil war started thousands of civilians sought safety in UN compounds in Juba, Bor, Akobo, Bentiu, Malakal and Melut. UNMISS had to adapt rapidly from a mission geared to build new state institutions to a mission providing protection to thousands of Internally Displaced People. Almost overnight, UNMISS also became responsible for the feeding, health and safety of the people under its care. At its height UNMISS was responsible for more than 200,000 people in Protection of Civilians (POC) sites in its compounds. The EPON report found that without the direct protection and broader actions undertaken by UNMISS, tens of thousands more people would have died during the civil war in South Sudan.

These developments radically changed the mission's role. In addition to protecting and caring for civilians, the UN also became responsible for monitoring and promoting human rights, for providing protection to and assisting humanitarian action, and for contributing to support the efforts to end the war. Once the peace agreements were signed in 2015 and 2019, UNMISS had an important additional role to support the Cease-fire Transitional Supporting Arrangement Mechanism (CTSAM) and the Joint Monitoring and Evaluation Commission (JMEC) with the implementation of these agreements.

In 2020, the arrival of the COVID-19 pandemic further exacerbated many of these vulnerabilities and contributed to delays in the implementation of the peace process. The capital Juba has been especially affected and several politicians, government officials, and international staff, including UN peacekeepers, had tested positive.

The independent review commissioned by the UN Security Council released its report in January 2021. It found that the R-ARCSS contained a clear vision for securing peace in South Sudan, but that its implementation has been slow and uneven. The review found that instead of prioritizing those elements of the agreement that would strengthen governance and accountability, the parties to the agreement focused on elite power-sharing arrangements. Importantly, the review concluded that although the R-ARCSS has been successful in reducing large-scale fighting and bringing most parties of the conflict into dialogue, it have not yet addressed the underlying drivers that triggered and fuelled civil war in South Sudan. The current peace process is thus still very fragile and the review recommended that the mission prioritizes actions to support the implementation of the peace agreement.

The UN Security Council considered the report of the independent review and the UN Secretary-General's recommendations and renewed the mandate of UNMISS for a year on 12 March 2021. Although the four core elements of the mandate remain unchanged, a number of specific tasks were added. For example, regarding the support to the peace process, the mission was tasked to share with the Security Council, by 15 July 2021, an assessment of what is needed to support the Government and creating an enabling environment for elections. New tasks also included strengthening the coordination with relevant regional actors like the Intergovernmental Authority on Development (IGAD) and the African Union (AU). The new mandate has also re-designated the POC sites as IDPs camps, signalling a change in posture for UNMISS and greater responsibility for UN and other humanitarian actors in managing these camps. The new mandate also tasks UNMISS to support the Government, through technical assistance and capacity building, to help build and reform the rule of law and justice institutions. The mission's work in this area was suspended when the civil war broke out, and this new element in the mandate thus represent the start of the return of the capacity building elements of the original UNMISS mandate.

The new resolution also strengthens the language on the adverse effects of climate change on the humanitarian situation and stability in South Sudan, and it task UNMISS (and urges the Government) to include climate-related security risks into its comprehensive risk assessments and risk management strategies. This is important because although the R-ARCSS has more-or-less brought large-scale fighting to an end, inter-communal conflict – which was a major cause of fatalities and displacement before the civil war – has significantly increased since 2019. These conflicts will be a major source of instability and displacement in the years ahead if the national, state and local governments and communities, with support from UNMISS and other international partners, are not able to prevent and manage these disputes before they turn violent.

The peace process in South Sudan is thus still highly vulnerable to relapse. Although the Revitalized Peace Agreement has brought large-scale fighting to an end, inter-communal conflict has flared up and will most likely be a major cause of instability and displacement in the year ahead. The implementation of the peace agreement has been slow and uneven with the parties mainly focused on elite power-sharing arrangements. In the mean-time, the corona virus (COVID-19) pandemic has contributed to delaying the full implementation of the peace agreement, and it has also disrupted the work of the United Nations (UN) which is in a new lockdown phase after several members of its staff tested positive.

The next year will thus be critical for South Sudan and UNMISS. UNMISS has an important role to play in supporting the Government, IGAD, the AU and other international partners to implement the peace agreement, to prevent and manage inter-communal conflict and to prevent and manage the spread of the COVID-19 pandemic.

UNMISS and Lessons on the Use of Force

The UNMISS experience to date has generated a number of lessons for the Use of Force, especially in the context of the Protection of Civilians mandate. Two in particular stand out, namely, whether it is realistic for a UN peacekeeping mission to use force against host nation forces, and what peacekeepers should do when faced with the choice of prioritizing protecting the few or the many.

The UN Protection of Civilians policy, and the specific mandate of UNMISS both state that the UN peacekeeping mission is responsible for protecting civilians in imminent threat of danger regardless of the threat. However, the reality in UN peacekeeping missions is that the mission's presence and legal status in a country is determined by a status of forces agreement with the host country. This agreement represents the political and legal consent of the host state to the presence and role of the mission.

A critical difference between peacekeeping and peace enforcement is the consent of the parties to a conflict, and especially that of the host nation. The Security Council can authorize an operation without the consent of the host nation, but that would then be a peace enforcement operation that is deployed with the expectation that it would be met with resistance. There are very few examples of such missions. The 1991 Gulf War to end the occupation of Kuwait by Iraq and the 1999 intervention of The International Force East Timor (INTERFET) to stop the war in East Timor comes to mind. As these two examples show, when it comes to peace enforcement operations the UN turns to coalitions of the willing because UN peacekeeping is not fit for combat operations. This is because the multinational command and control structure, the fractured combination of forces and the equipment of a UN peacekeeping mission works very well for peacekeeping, but it is not fit for the purpose of combat operations. Effective combat operations require a level of unity of command, shared doctrine and an interoperability of forces that is usually only achieved within a national defence force or among countries that share a common defence culture and that are used to operating together.

However, the expectation that a UN peacekeeping force will use force against a host nation to protect civilians can raise very similar challenges, depending on the nature of the specific incident. In the case of South Sudan, the Sudan People's Liberation Army (SPLA) have been engaged in a 20-year civil war with the Government of Sudan before independence. After independence the SPLA have been transformed into the national army, and since 2013 the SPLA have been engaged in a civil war within South Sudan with the SPLM-IO and other break away factions. In addition to battle-hardened troops the armed forces are experienced in using heavy equipment like tanks, artillery and attack helicopters. The armed forces of South Sudan thus have formidable capabilities. If the peacekeeping mission becomes engaged in an armed confrontation with the armed forces of South Sudan to protect civilians the situation can potentially escalate and result in a larger confrontation that could have disastrous consequences for the UN and the people it is mandated to protect.

The experience of UNMISS thus raise the question of whether it is militarily and politically realistic to mandate a peacekeeping operation to use force to protect civilians against a host state. In the case of UNMISS the mission leadership and command structure, down to the tactical level, have to make life and death choices on a daily basis to try and balance the demands of the mandate and the expectation that the mission should be able to protect all civilians, even when the perpetrators are host nation forces. They have to balance the risk to the people they are mandated to protect and themselves, and the risk to maintaining consent of the mission overall, should a specific action to protect civilians result in a larger confrontation.

The UN's Protection of Civilians policy consists of three tiers, namely protection through dialogue, physical protection and protection through creating an enabling environment. The UNMISS experience has shown that when it comes to protecting civilians against potential harm from Government forces, the first and third tiers are the most effective and realistic. As the EPON study cited above and others have determined, UNMISS has been able to protect tens of thousands of civilians through its POC cites and it has contributed to protecting thousands more via its presence, and its monitoring and reporting function, as well as by engaging in political dialogue with the parties at all levels. However, physically protecting civilians against host nation forces has only been possible when individual soldiers or small groups of soldiers have threatened civilians in their personal capacities. When government forces act purposefully to attack civilians, or if civilians are harmed as a side-effect of fighting between government forces and rebels, intervention by the peacekeeping mission is interpreted as action in support of the opposing forces and this has had significant political costs.

Even if the situation is contained tactically, it could escalate politically, and it could ultimately result in the country withdrawing consent, and then the peacekeeping mission will have to leave the country. Peacekeepers are thus frequently faced with an ethical dilemma, do they act to protect the few civilians in imminent danger, even if that action can escalate and threaten the thousands of civilians they are protecting in their POC sites, or even the consent of the mission itself. If the mission has to withdraw the approximately two hundred thousand IDPs the mission is protecting at its POC sites will be left unprotected. A small firefight during a patrol can escalate, and as peacekeepers retreat into their base it can draw the fight to the base, and it can result in considerable harm to the civilians sheltering in the POC site as well as the civilian, police and military peacekeepers in the base. Peacekeepers, at all levels, but frequently at the tactical level, are thus faced with decisions that can have significant tactical, operational and even strategic consequences. Framed in these terms, the caution that many peacekeeping commanders exercise, and for which peacekeeping is often criticised, can perhaps be better understood.

There are several solutions. The UNMISS experience suggest that one option is to be much clearer when it comes to under what circumstances peacekeepers can use physical violence to protect civilians if the perpetrators are host nation armed forces. Another is that peacekeeping commanders at all levels, but especially at tactical level, needs much more training to prepare them for dealing with the kind of use of force and POC decisions they will be forced to make on a daily basis. They also need to be empowered to make much more use of tier 1 (dialogue) and tier 3 (enabling environment) instruments, in order to minimize the need for tier 2 (physical protection) actions, as these always involve risk for the other civilians the mission is tasked to protect, the mission and the peacekeepers themselves. For example, if the risk to civilians around a POC site is mainly caused by host nation soldiers acting in their personal capacity, then dialogue with local commanders and agreed protocols for responding to such incidents can significantly reduce the chances for misunderstanding and escalation. Similarly, an assessment of the POC risks for civilians can assist with tier 3 actions which can reduce exposure to risk. For example, instead of civilians individually collecting water or firewood, escorting patrols can be organized to accompany groups of civilians to offer them protection.

Conclusion

UNMISS thus provides us with a host of lessons that can be used to streamline and improve how and when UN peacekeeping missions use force to protect civilians. Greater clarity is needed regarding the options that peacekeepers have when it comes to protecting civilians when the danger is posed by host nation forces. And more guidance should be provided to peacekeepers when it comes to choices between protecting the few versus the many.

Relevance of The Principle of Use of Force: The Case of MONUSCO

Lieutenant General Chander Prakash, SM, VSM (Retd)

Background and Nature of Conflict

Post-independence from Belgium on 30 June 1960, eastern portion of the Democratic Republic of Congo (DRC) has been through series of long, complex, and brutal conflicts. The First Congo War (1996–1997), also nicknamed Africa's First World War, was a civil war and an international military conflict which took place mostly in the DRC (then Zaire), had major spill over into Sudan and Uganda. In this war, Rwanda and Uganda defeated then President Mobutu Sese Seko and supported Laurent Kabila to become the President in May 1997. This was followed by the Second Congo War (1998-1999) between Rwanda and Uganda vs DRC, Angola and Zimbabwe in which a number of Armed Groups emerged in the eastern DRC. Conflict in the DRC has continued since then with its nature and intensity varying from time to time.

In 2013, there were roughly 70 armed groups operating in the eastern DRC. Now it is believed that this number has reduced to dozens. These armed groups have diverse motivations from protecting the interests of various ethnic groups, political supporters and local communities to even wanting to establish an Islamic state in Uganda. They often fight each other and the Congolese armed forces (Forces Armées de la République Démocratique du Congo or FARDC). Their alliances and animosities keep changing. Some of the armed groups receive covert/overt support from the neighbouring states, which complicates the matter.

The conflict in the DRC is characterised by widespread, systematic, and brutal targeting of the local civilians. Looting, sexual violence, forced labour, kidnapping, forced recruitment including of children are frequent occurrence. Rapes are used as weapon of war. Sad and unfortunate are the rapes that took place in the Walikale territory of North Kivu Province over a period of four days – from 30 July to 2 August 2010 – wherein 300 women, 55 girls, 23 men, and 9 boys, were systematically raped and subjected to other forms of sexual violence by one of the armed groups.

The operations of the armed group are sustained through the exploitation of the country's natural resources, which are in abundance in the eastern DRC, and by violent coercion and exploitation of civilian population. According to a recent report by the United Nations Environment Programme, "the protracted conflict cycle and insecurity in eastern DRC appear increasingly dominated by economic interests rather than predominantly political motivations".

In addition to illegal the exploitation of natural resources, the armed groups resort to taxation of businesses, market taxes, household taxes, and sometimes outright looting. The long and brutal conflict in the DRC has caused massive suffering for civilians, with estimates of millions dead (some estimate the number to be as high as six million) either directly or indirectly as a result of the fighting. United Nations Office for the Coordination of Humanitarian Affairs had reported that the number of Internally Displaced Persons in the DRC had risen to 3.8 million in 2017, the highest in

Africa.[1] This is the scale and nature of misery that the DRC has been/is going through, which needs to be addressed by the peacekeepers in uniform and civil.

Principles of UN Peacekeeping As Applied in the DRC

Three basic principles of peacekeeping, as these have evolved over a period of time, are *consent of the parties to the conflict, impartiality,* and *use of force in self-defence and in support of the mandate.* These are meant to balance the Member States' sovereignty and the United Nations. However, as the nature of conflict has changed from interstate to intrastate, these have been applied in UN peace operations particularly in the DRC, keeping in mind the spirit of the principles but with the primary intent not to impinge on the sovereignty and to ensure protection of civilians.

In the DRC, since it is an intrastate conflict involving armed groups and confined to the national borders, it is neither feasible nor desirable to obtain the consent of all parties to the conflict. Therefore, the consent of the main party to the conflict i.e. the national government exists. However, the mission's political freedom of action is anything but guaranteed in the DRC. This, to an extent, is a compromise of the principle of 'impartiality'. For the Military Component of the Mission, the principle of 'impartiality' is non-negotiable and sacrosanct to maintain the creditability of the United Nations on the ground.

The Capstone Doctrine notes that UN peacekeepers could punish any party that fails to respect the peace agreement that the peacekeeping force is meant to protect. Such parties as 'spoilers', defined as individuals or groups that may profit from the spread or continuation of violence,

---

1   UNOCHA website. Available at https://www.unocha.org/fr/story/drc-number-internally-displaced-people-rises-38-million-highest-africa. Accessed on 20 February 2021.

or have an interest to disrupt a resolution of a conflict in a given setting permits use of force. From a legal point of view, impartiality may or may not be a requirement, depending on the legal basis upon which the resolution is taken. Nevertheless, it is still vital that the parties conceive the operation impartial.

Impartiality implies that a peacekeeping operation must implement its mandate without favour or prejudice to any party. This should not be confused with neutrality or inactivity. UN peacekeepers should be impartial in their dealings with the parties to the conflict, but not neutral in the execution of their mandate. The mission in DRC cannot close its eyes to wrong doings of DRC's security forces. FARDC and the national police have in the past have been responsible for human rights violations including rapes. Being poorly paid and not disciplined tend to prey on the population. Human Rights Due Diligence Policy (HRDDP) of the UN is intended to address this issue. But, it has thrown up different challenges.

Use of Force

MONUC / MONUSCO in the absence of the ability of the national government in the DRC to protect civilians, has been authorised to 'Use of Force' in support of the mandate which includes protection of civilians by the peacekeepers. Protection of civilians is a priority task of the mission since 2008.

UN forces in the DRC have been using force since the 1960s in different contexts and constellations. However, peacekeepers' right to use force has been under constant development, and the legal basis for this practice has often been far from clear due to the political character of the subject. As a result, although the core principles may be generally accepted in practice, the boundaries delimiting the principles remain controversial. Some argue that robust military engagement is vital for the UN in order for it to carry out its tasks effectively. Others hold the view that the UN's use of force beyond self-defence is inconsistent with the UN's Charter and its principles. Even if the UN should go on proactive and be on the offensive as has been the case wrt Force Intervention Brigade in the DRC, the question remains: to what extent it is practical and will it achieve long lasting peace? MONUSCO from 2010 onwards has used force to a varying degree from the tactical level to the strategic level. An analysis of the same is in the succeeding paragraphs.

In July 2010, there was a demand from the Congolese Government to draw down the mission as they felt that the security situation had improved. But the Security Council felt otherwise and a compromise was arrived at. MONUC was renamed as MONUSCO to focus on stabilizing the eastern DRC, protection of civilians and eventually draw down. That meant institutions building, Security Sector Reforms and nation building. Regrettably, even today, the situation in eastern DRC has not fully stabilized and the civilians continue to be under threat.

MONUSCO military and police component in 2010 and 2011 had adopted a deterrent posture to protect civilians under eminent threat. MONUSCO was encouraging and supporting the National Army (FARDC) to launch military operations against the armed groups, especially the FDLR and Mayi Mayi Groups. MONUSCO provided protection umbrella to the civilians in most vulnerable areas. These measures, in a slow and steady manner were yielding positive results. In country like the DRC, where there are hardly any roads, many inaccessible areas and limited air mobility means with the mission, this is a daunting task. But the expectations in some quarters were very high and therefore fell short of expectations.

Turning point came when the national elections were held in the DRC in November 2011. These were not perceived as fair and lacked creditability. This contributed to the birth of 23 March Movement (M23). The M23 was formed on 4 April 2012 when nearly 300 soldiers - the majority of them former members of the National Congress for the Defence of the People (CNDP) - turned against the DRC government citing poor conditions in the army and the government›s unwillingness to implement the 23 March 2009 peace deal. A United Nations report found that Rwanda created and commanded the M23 rebel group.[2]

M23 kept occupying various villages and towns in North Kivu Province and finally M23 rebels advanced on Goma, provincial capital of North Kivu on 20 November 2012. The Congolese Army retreated from their positions with little fighting or no resistance at all. The National Army, even though supported by MONUSCO both operationally and logistically, was not willing to fight and proved incapable of stopping the advance of M23. M23 forces paraded through the city of Goma, the provincial capital of North Kivu, and many residents turned out to welcome them. MONUSCO actively patrolled the area in spite of M23's presence and greatly contributed to the prevent Human Rights violations. A story that is never told as good news, as media only picks up but bad news as it sells. There was also lack of strategic communications on part of MONUSCO. In such a scenario, should MONUSCO have used force and resultant collateral damage is a moot question.

Authorisation of Force Intervention Brigade

The regional organisations such as ICGLR, SADC and AU who were troubled by instability in DRC approached the

---

2   French W. Howard.   The Case Against Rwanda' President Paul Kagame *Newsweek*. 02 March 2021. Accessed on 03 March 2021.

United Nations Security Council (UNSC) to take decisive action in the DRC against the Armed Groups in particular against M23 and FDLR. These regional organisations had themselves been discussing creating an Intervention Brigade to deal with the situation. UN under pressure from various quarters needed to gain control over the situation. UNSC, on 28 March 2013 through Resolution 2098 authorised the deployment of the Force Intervention Brigade (FIB). *This brigade was empowered to carry out targeted offensive operations either unilaterally or jointly with the FARDC, in a robust, highly mobile and versatile manner and in strict compliance with international law, including international humanitarian law, and was tasked to prevent the expansion of all armed groups, neutralise these groups, and to disarm them in order to contribute to the objective of reducing the threat posed by armed groups on state authority and civilian security in eastern DRC and to make space for stabilisation activities.*

This was an unprecedented mandate with appropriate resources given by the UNSC to any UN peacekeeping mission. MONUSCO has been the first UN peacekeeping mission which was sanctioned first-ever 'offensive' combat force in the form of FIB, intended to carry out targeted operations to 'neutralise and disarm' the M23, as well as 'other Congolese rebels and foreign rebel groups in strife-driven eastern Democratic Republic of Congo. The FIB consists of three Infantry Battalions, one Artillery Battery and one Special Force and Reconnaissance Company. It was supported by the state of art South African Attack Helicopters and drones. The force consists of troops from Tanzania, South Africa and Malawi. Whereas traditional UN peacekeepers are armed with light weapons intended for use in self-defence, but the Intervention Brigade is equipped with an array of weapons such as mortars, snipers, heavy artillery and, crucially, attack helicopters to press the offensive against Congolese rebels. It was a shift away from traditional peacekeeping and towards peace enforcement.

Operations of Force Intervention Brigade

By November 2013, about eight months from the authorisation of FIB by UNSC, M23's leader then, Sultani Makenga, and 1,700 fighters fled to Uganda, where they surrendered and were disarmed. Starting January 2014, after the defeat of M23, the Intervention Brigade in tandem with FARDC conducted operations directed against the Allied Democratic Forces (ADF), an Islamist group that originated in western Uganda and other armed groups. The ADF is a potent armed group and has been operating in the eastern DRC for decades. They have carried out a string of horrific attacks against civilians and are blamed for the kidnapping of roughly 1,000 civilians over the last so many years. Only partial success has been achieved against this group. ADF continues to target civilians and FARDC and even UN peacekeepers to date and remains a major driver of insecurity in the Ituri Region.

MONUSCO's operations against smaller rebel groups jointly with FARDC or otherwise, with the offensive military capabilities provided to the FIB have proven to be reasonably effective in eliminating the threat posed to the civilians. Conversely, the FARDC operations against the FDLR, carried out without the help of MONUSCO's drones, artillery, and helicopters, have not been as successful as those carried out with MONUSCO's backing. Thus, the FDLR continues to threaten local civilian population. The military operations show a record of mixed success, and highlight the need for cooperation between the UN and host governments in order to be effective.

Analysis of Use of Force at Tactical and Strategic Level

As a benevolent criticism, it can be argued that the faith in peacekeeping had to be kept intact and therefore the exceptional situation in eastern Congo called for exceptional and unprecedented measures to be taken. But, legally speaking, the MONUSCO became a party to the conflict regardless of the Government's consent, since it is mandated to take action against specific groups. In reality, it compromised the UN's ability to be impartial. It is very difficult to derive any definitive conclusions about the long-term effect of use of force at the strategic level on civilian protection. Each case of conflict will have to be examined on its own to determine if and when the FIB model would be effective given the specific context. Some take always from the FIB model are:-

> There may be some justification of application of FIB model in the case where the armed groups commit atrocities and abuse the civilians for mustering their resources. But it is unlikely to be any worthwhile justification for use of force at the strategic level for combating voluntarily supported armed groups. This would necessitate a more wide ranging counterinsurgency strategy, requiring more resources than is feasible for UN deployments.

> The FIB was operational in about three months' time which is seldom the case in UN deployments. In this case, the regional organizations such as the International Conference on the Great Lakes Region, South African Development Community and the African Union who were concerned by insecurity created, expressed support for an offensive intervention against armed groups in the eastern DRC prior to the Security Council's authorisation of the FIB. This resulted in speedy deployment with the necessary wherewithal and the political will to undertake offensive operations.

➢ Identifying member states with the military capacity and political will to contribute to an FIB intervention prior to its authorization significantly reduced the deployment time and a clear and a strong message to the targeted group (M23). This tilted the balance of power against in favour of national authorities.

➢ When measuring the success of an operation from the perspective of civilian protection, simple victory over an armed group is not enough. Target groups need to be neutralised decisively and quickly for continued and long term protection of civilians. Otherwise, they are likely to re-emerge and target the civilians for having supported the government/UN Forces.

➢ Without the adequate and suitable resources to quickly overcome a targeted group, military operations against said group have the potential to increase the danger to civilians. Unfortunately, this seems to have been the case in the operations against the ADF. The failure to decisively defeat the group allowed it to increase its violence against civilians in the Ituri district.

➢ In situations where multiple armed groups constitute a threat to civilian populations, an overwhelming victory against some of them is likely to refrain others from targeting civilians and they may abandon armed conflict and come to the negotiating table. Conversely, a weak peace enforcement operation against a targeted group (s) is unlikely to have an adequate robust deterrent effect. Thus mitigating one of the major benefits such a strategy may hold for civilian protection.

➢ One of the valuable lessons learned in the DRC is that no amount of offensive military capabilities can be effective if the forces are unable to locate targeted groups, move and deploy and act quickly against them and thereafter carry out sustained operations. Surveillance and intelligence capabilities (both imagery and human) are particularly vital. Insufficient intelligence creates the potential for increased danger to civilians as there could be misapplication of force and resultant collateral damage.

➢ In order to carry out rapid and effective operations against the targeted groups, the military force will need to be equipped with mobile offensive capabilities such as the attack helicopters, transportation resources and also supporting logistics.

Host Government's Actions Post Intervention by the UN Forces

One of the inherent effects of successful UN intervention is the expansion of the state's territorial control. In order to ensure that the intervention is effective not only in ending armed groups' operations but it also improves the safety of civilians in the long run, the host government's potential to control and administer the area post intervention by the UN Forces is important. Else resurgence of violence against civilians by the armed groups is a good possibility.

Another possibility, which should not be lost sight of, is that after the government forces regain its authority then they may commit violence against the civilians. Therefore, unless appropriate measures are taken in advance in consultation with the host, UN intervention may simply deliver civilians from the hands of one abuser into those of another. Some have criticised the Intervention Brigade's deployment in the eastern DRC and the UN's military cooperation with the FARDC on the grounds that they are collaborating with government forces which have been abusing civilians themselves.

Conclusion

No doubt that the UN authorisation and deployment of the FIB in the DRC has been a milestone in UN peace operations but it has serious ramifications and related issues that need to be simultaneously addressed as have been discussed above. Use of force at the strategic level challenges some of the core notions of the traditional model of UN peacekeeping operations, and introduces the possibility of using more robust peace enforcement strategies in the UN's efforts to improve the security of civilian populations. Such strategies have the potential to improve civilian protection by deterring and disarming, or even demobilising the armed groups. But then there are other serious issues that also need to be thought over. The Intervention Brigade initial success in proactively combating armed groups through an offensive mandate and military capabilities is reason for cautious optimism. However, it needs to be noted that the initial military success has not been effective in reducing overall levels of violence against civilians. Like any tool, the FIB model should only be applied in cases it is best suited for and that too for a defined period of time. The FIB model should be considered as a politico-military tool for a short time and should not raise expectations that it will protect all civilians all of the time. Ultimately, for long term and lasting improvements in civilian security, political solutions have to be explored.

Contribution of UNDOF for Sustainable Peace

Lieutenant General IS Singha, AVSM, VSM (Retd)

Introduction

United Nations Disengagement and Observer Force (UNDOF) was established on 31 May 1974 at Golan Heights between Israel and Syria, as per Security Council Resolution 350 (1974), after the 1973 Yom Kippur War between Israel and its Arab neighbours. The mission operated from a number of Observation Points (OPs) located on high ground manned by the military observers (MILOBS) and positions manned by Troop Contributing Country (TCCs) along the road axes on either side of the buffer zone called the Area of Separation. UNDOF is a small mission, one tenth in size when compared to the neighbouring mission in Lebanon (UNIFIL), with around 1000 uniformed peacekeepers, 50 odd international staff and about 100 local staff members. These men and women were sufficient to oversee the ceasefire, in normal times, and report any violations to the Ceasefire Agreement of 1974. The mission did not have a formal mechanised Force Reserve Company, Situational Awareness capabilities, anti-IED capability, Political advisors and a Deputy Force Commander (DFC). The civilian security organisation was also very limited with only two staff members.

As per the 1974 Ceasefire Agreement, no armed troops of the two parties to the conflict, Israel or Syria, were allowed to come into the buffer zone; called the Area of Separation (AOS). This AOS is 75 km long along the front in a funnel shape; is approximately 10 km wide in the North and 01 km wide in the South. 25 km on either side of the AOS is Area of Limitation (AOL), where limited number of troops and weapons are allowed to be deployed by the parties. This arrangement was generally respected by both the parties for nearly four decades and any inadvertent or intentional violation was flagged at the UN HQ level in the weekly report. The three principals of peacekeeping, namely; **Consent, Impartiality and No use of Force** were easily implemented.

A traditional interstate mission between Israel and Syria went awry and its complexion changed with advent of Arab Spring. With the start of the Civil War in Syria in 2011, certain Armed Opposition Groups (AOGs) came into the AOS since it was considered the safest region in Syria. To contest these armed groups, Syrian Arab Armed Forces (SAAF) troops also entered the buffer zone. Both sides were in possession of heavier weapons including automatics, rocket launchers, tanks and artillery guns. They entrenched themselves into make shift posts and started manning check posts leading to their posts. The roles of the UN and Syrians were reversed wherein SAAF and AOGs started checking the movement of UN peacekeepers and the civilians in the buffer zone; a task hither-to-fore being performed by the peacekeepers to ensure armed troops/irregulars from both sides, Israel and Syria, were not allowed to enter the buffer zone. The traditional inter-state mission also became intra-state and complex in nature.

Operational Environment

On a daily basis, peacekeepers started coming under crossfire, were subjected to carjacking and weapon snatching and their freedom of movement was largely restricted. Since some UN vehicles including the bullet proof ones were taken away by force, by AOGs as well as pro-government militia groups, their rampant use to misguide the other side was resorted to. Within our capabilities, we started giving medical cover to all wounded persons who reported to peacekeeper observation posts or positions without a weapon. Presence of 30 odd Armed Opposition Groups (AOGs) including ISIS affiliates in mission area complicated the situation as they were not signatories to the 1974 Agreement but hindered and endangered peacekeeping operations. Two Internally Displaced Persons (IDP) camps came up; one in the North and the other in the South of the AOS. Inadequacy of the Mandate and mission capabilities to meet the developing situation was highly pronounced.

The Mission leadership took a considered decision to open the lines of communication with the local population and the SAAF commanders in the field; both considered a taboo by the Syrian Govt which did not want international forces to come in contact with their population for the fear that the border area population may not get subverted. These lines of communications were considered paramount for the UN force to ensure own safety, the need for actionable intelligence, as also to dispel certain misconceptions of the intent and actions of the peacekeepers in a very fluid and dynamic environment. The local and vernacular media blamed UN for taking sides and helping the government troops in movement, operations and logistic backup. The Syrian government felt that the UN was soft and tilted towards the AOGs and assisting them with arms, ammunition, medical cover and conveyance.

Mandate

The mandate of UNDOF is the shortest in the history of UN peacekeeping as compared to the other 70 odd peacekeeping missions. The one sentence mandate reads: **Maintain credible presence in Golan and use its best efforts to maintain the ceasefire between Israel and Syrian Arab Republic and see to it that it is scrupulously observed.** The short mandate had both advantages as well as disadvantages. Whereas the mandate does not include details of how to achieve ceasefire and retain it, it also gives the mission inherence flexibility to do certain actions in good faith. For example, the mission is not mandated for protection of civilians and provision of rations, water and medical aid to the civilians in a state of emergency. Keeping the preamble of United Nations **to save successive generations of mankind from the scourge of war** in mind, we were able to extend some facilities to the civilians in exceptional circumstances. As access to ICRC and other humanitarian organisations were denied to the forward areas as also areas under domination of the opposition groups by the Syrian government, the mission undertook some operations like provision of polio drops to the newly born babies and water supply and medical cover to the improvised IDP camps.

Consent

Ever since May 1974, when the Ceasefire Agreement was signed, the mandate had to be extended by Security Council every six months in the end of June and December. As per the Agreement, Syria was the host nation and as such, all logistic chains functioned from the Syrian side. Due to the prevailing unrest, logistic chains were often disrupted and snapped for prolonged periods creating logistical and operational challenges for the mission. The host government was also responsible for the security of the peacekeepers, the lever that I used with my interlocutor in all our meetings. The consent of both the parties, Israel and Syria was a pre-requisite for the Security Council to finally issue a resolution extending the mission by six months. The main consideration and instrument of decision making, of course, was based on the recommendations of the mission leadership. Till the beginning of the Arab Spring, the six monthly extension of the mandate was a routine activity but with the advent of the Syrian Civil war in 2011, the fear and uncertainty of whether the Syrian Government will be in power or out of it for the next six months' renewal of the mandate was always looming large over the decision making of the mission leadership.

With both AOGs and SAAF being deployed in the buffer zone (AOS) the mission leadership had to open the lines of communication with all opposite groups including the Syrian Free Army to ensure that in the eventuality of their coming to power, they were well disposed towards the mission, knew the importance of continuation of the mission and would willingly give their consent if they came to power. At the same time, the mission leadership had to maintain a balance and keep the incumbent government in good humour and retain their confidence, so that in spite of the fragile internal situation, they gave their consent if they were still calling the shots. The peacekeepers and the mission leadership had to do a tight rope walk to ensure that they continued to fulfil the mandate; retain the confidence of all parties as also their freedom of movement and strike a balance in the mission area.

Our liaison capabilities had to be tripled in order to keep in touch with not only the two parties, Israel and Syria, who were signatories to the agreement, but also with 30 odd AOG groups who were not the signatories but were creating daily security challenges for the peacekeepers. The periodicity of meetings with various parties had also increased manifold due to enhanced violent incidents taking place in the mission area. Sometimes, to diffuse the situation I had to engage all parties and move from the mission area to Damascus and Tel Aviv and back on the same day.

Impartiality

With the security situation being in a state of flux and the ground situation changing dynamically, in the prevailing milieu and the melee, the impartiality of the peacekeepers came under deep scrutiny. Five out of the six original TCCs except for India, pulled out their troops quoting security reasons but actually for domestic and international political implications. In the prevailing dynamic security situation, retaining impartiality and still be able to fulfil the mandate was one of the greatest challenges in the mission area.

Since the Syrian Government was resorting to barrel bombing of the areas under the domination of the opposition forces as also subjecting these areas to artillery and mortar bombs, the peacekeepers witnessed lots of casualties to innocent civilians including women and children and their movement to improvised IDP camps. These people were always in need of food, water, shelter and essential medical cover and the mission always chipped in with the few resources at hand. When these incidents were flagged to our Syrian interlocutor, a Brigadier General from the Engineers called the Senior Syrian Arab Delegate (SSAD), his normal reaction was that it was an internal affair of Syria and the peacekeepers should not be bothered for their population as it was not part of mandate. He would add that the responsibility of looking after the civilians was that of their government and it was doing its best efforts which were interrupted and dwarfed by actions of armed opposition groups.

The mission leadership also opened up regular communication channels with the AOGs, much against the wishes of the Syrian Government. Leaders of the AOGs always accused us of not doing enough to lessen the miseries of the population and siding with the government. We had to get down to the levels of these leaders who were at times half literate and explain our position that we were not deployed to bring peace to the internal strife of Syria but to ensure that Syria and Israel did not go to war again. Our resources were limited but we were still flagging all violent incidents initiated from all sides and in a way informing the world through UN Security Council of the actual events taking place in the mission area. It was very difficult to justify what we were doing but eventually we were always able to pacify and reassure all the opposition groups that we were not taking sides and our sympathies were with the population since they were facing the wrath of both the Syrian security forces (SAAF) and the AOGs.

As stated earlier, AOGs and government pro militia groups forcefully took away some vehicles from the peacekeepers and started misusing them for their own logistic and operational needs. The movement of these vehicles was always spotted by the posts and improvised barriers set up by the AOGs and the SAAF and they accused UN for siding with the other side. UN became the whipping boy of both the sides and it took great amount of perseverance and convincing on our part to ensure both the AOGs and the SAAF that the peacekeepers would never ever facilitate the movement of war like stores and logistic chains meant for any type of armed bodies on the Syrian side. SAAF went a step ahead to use their military police vehicles which were painted white to confuse and lull the AOGs, thinking it was a UN troop movement and open fire onto those groups once they closed in on them. We had to lodge protests vehemently, time and again, with our Syrian interlocutor, SSAD; to put an end to such practices wherein the blame comes unfairly onto the peacekeepers.

The Israelis seemingly did not want to interfere in the internal affairs of Syria but made all efforts to woo the local Syrian population in the AOS because they felt that mindful of any outcome of the civil war in Syria, they would eventually have to deal with this population for posterity. At the behest of the mission leadership the Israelis started augmenting our efforts in provision of medical aid to the innocent civilians who became casualties, since they were not able to go to hospitals in Syria and were way beyond our capability to handle. There was a heated debate between higher echelons of the IDF whether to take on this responsibility or to stay aloof. Whereas the IDF Headquarters and CDS Benny Gantz felt they should not interfere in the internal affairs of Syrians, the Army Commanders in the field including Gen Golan, the Northern Army Commander and a local, felt that it was the best way to win the hearts and minds of the border population, which was artificially divided on both sided of the ceasefire line. We supported the local commanders and prevailed over the IDF Headquarters but also clarified our position that in order to retain our impartiality between the two parties Syria and Israel, we will not be able to support them openly. In due course the Israelis set up a field hospital on their side of the ceasefire line and we overlooked who all were being treated in those hospitals. I also worked closely with ICRC on both sides to coordinate their efforts to provide medical assistance to locals, an action which was way beyond our mandate.

No Use of Force

Since the mission was under Chapter VI and not Chapter VII, force was never used by peacekeepers ever since the inception of the mission in 1974. Therefore, the movement from one place to the other was never a tactical movement. Although the peacekeepers less the Observers always carried their personal weapons with them, they were carried more in an administrative manner, sometimes even kept in the boot. Therefore, if challenged or fired upon by any group of armed men, peacekeepers were not in a position to use their weapons instantly and return the fire. Some over cautious commanders of the TCCs did not even allot ammunition to their troops in order to avoid accidental fire. Not a single round had been fired between Israelis and Syrians for nearly four decades and the lives of peacekeepers were never threatened till the beginning of the civil war. It took great amount of effort to shed the defensive mind set and make the peacekeepers move tactically and be in position to fire back instantaneously.

The first time the peacekeepers fired back at the AOGs was when one of our positions became inaccessible due to blocking of the road by AOGs who wanted to deter SAAF troops to advance towards their stronghold nearby. The policy put in place was that a position would not be allowed to be isolated for more than 48 hours. I tasked the Phillipino CO to personally lead a strong patrol to open the axis to one of his isolated positions next to a village (Position 69). As the peacekeepers tried to negotiate the road block and open the road, they were fired upon by AOGs. The CO immediately ordered for return of fire. Suddenly, the AOGs came out with a white flag urging us to ceasefire and they also made it clear that they had no intention to fight the UN peacekeepers.

Assertive Peacekeeping

The mission leadership had to sensitise the international and local staff of the existential threats. The uniformed peacekeepers working under their TCC leadership were more successful in adapting to the changed environment than their civilian counterparts. With the help of UN Headquarters, New York, a Mission Capability Study was ordered to ensure Capacity Building in Command and Control, liaison, protection, situational awareness, security and anti IED capability.

All movement of troops, international and national staff, was controlled and on Syrian side was part of a convoy movement with protection. The troops were made to move tactically so that they were in a position to use their weapons with ease in a desired time frame. Automatics were mounted and manned on vehicles more as a deterrence but also in a ready position to return fire if fired upon. We actually wanted to call it Robust Peacekeeping, but UN Headquarters urged us not use the term as we were operating under Chapter VI. We finally settled down with the term Assertive Peacekeeping although in practice we were doing Robust Peacekeeping.

Conclusion

The Syrian Civil War resulted in changing the complexion of a traditional and pacific peacekeeping mission into a very challenging and dynamic one. Since the Security Council was divided over the Syrian crisis, getting a fresh and robust mandate on the lines of UNIFIL after 2005 war was rendered impossible. The mission had to evolve while coping up with the changed environment. The most challenging task was to change the mind set of peacekeepers who had seen better times in the mission area and the host nation. Evolving continuously with the changing environment was the key to survival and we were able to stay ahead of the situation.

Contribution of UNIFIL for Sustainable Peace

*Lieutenant General Jai Prakash Nehra, PVSM, AVSM** (Retd)*

Background

Over the years there has been a lot of debate on whether traditional peace keeping operations have been successful in sustaining peace in the conflict zones. On one hand contributions by UN Peacekeeping forces have been recognised by many in various ways, including the Nobel Prize in 1988, they have also been criticised on the other, perhaps rightly so since some missions like Bosnia and Rwanda did fail. What most critics fail to point out is that reasons for failure of a mission rarely lie at the doorstep of peacekeepers. Lack of commitment of the parties to the conflict to keep their word and honour UN Resolution(s) as also the inability of the international community to tackle the root cause of the conflict perhaps are the top two reasons for mission failures.

United Nations Interim Force in Lebanon (UNIFIL) too has got its share of criticism despite the peacekeepers performing commendably against all odds. One of the oldest UN Peacekeeping Missions, UNIFIL is deployed in one of the most sensitive regions of the world. Since its establishment in Mar 1978, the Mission has seen many ups and downs. Basically, a Chapter VI Mission, its initial mandate was to '*Confirm the withdrawal of Israeli forces from southern Lebanon, Restore international peace and security and Assist the Government of Lebanon in ensuring the return of its effective authority in the area (UNSCR 425)*'. Since then, the mandate has undergone many a change, major one being through UNSCR 1701 after the 2006 Israel – Hezbollah Conflict.

UNSCR 1701 authorised increase in UNIFIL's strength from 2000 to 15000 peacekeepers and made the mandate more robust. In addition to its existing mandate, it authorised UNIFIL '*to take all necessary action to ensure that its AO is not utilized for hostile activities of any kind, to resist attempts by forceful means to prevent it from discharging its duties under the mandate of the Security Council, and to protect United Nations personnel, facilities, installations and equipment, ensure the security and freedom of movement of UN personnel, humanitarian workers and, without prejudice to the responsibility of the Government of Lebanon, to protect civilians under imminent threat of physical violence*'.

Post UNSCR 1701, UNIFIL was strongly equipped with Main Battle Tanks (MBTs) and Artillery guns. There was also a strong European participation with France, Italy and Spain contributing fully equipped infantry battalions, besides others. A unique feature of UNIFIL was that it was authorised a Maritime Task Force (MTF), a flotilla that initially comprised over 15 ships including five frigates and 10 fast patrol boats, that enabled UNIFIL to ensure peace in the Lebanese territorial waters.

UNIFIL and Complex Lebanese Politics

UNIFIL operates in a sensitive and complex environment. The complexities need to be understood in the backdrop of orientation of and relationship between various stake holders such as the Israeli and Lebanese Establishment, Lebanese Armed Force (LAF) as well as non-state actors like Hezbollah and Palestinian armed groups.

Lebanon is a multi-party confession-oriented democracy. Home to 18 different religious sects, the main ones are Shia Muslims (27%), Sunni Muslims (27%) and Maronite Christians (21%). The constitution stipulates that the President be a Maronite Christian, Prime Minister a Sunni and the Speaker a Shia. The Chief of LAF too, customarily, is a Maronite Christian. Population of South Lebanon (UNIFIL AO) is predominantly Shia and has a strong presence of Hezbollah. Lebanese people are warm, friendly, and peace-loving with strong business acumen. They have a large expat population, approximately 14 million by some estimates, as against just about five M living within Lebanon. The expats live mainly in Latin America, Africa, and Europe. While the Lebanese consider Israel as enemy, their military has seldom confronted the Israel Defence Forces (IDF). Even during the days of Israeli Syrian occupation of Beirut, most resistance against Israel came mainly from non-state actors like Hezbollah and Amal. Even though it is an Arab nation, Lebanese are mostly of Levant descent and there is a strong French influence owing to the colonial past. Lebanese people tolerate the presence of Palestinian refugees but are not overly fond of them since most of their woes stem from hostile action by Palestinian armed groups against Israel and consequent Israeli retaliation.

Lebanese Army though not so well equipped or trained, is courageous, highly patriotic and much respected by the people. It has been instrumental in maintaining peace within the country and has given a good account fighting Islamic terrorists, notable one being their nearly four-month long fight with Fatah-al-Islam terrorists in Nahr-el-Bared, a Palestinian refugee camp near Tripoli. However, they do not act against Hezbollah fighters whom they term as the 'Resistance'.

Hezbollah, or the *Party of God* as they call themselves, are a highly motivated group of Muslim (mainly Shia) fighters with a strong leadership. Backed by Iran and Syria, they play a dominant role in internal politics and enjoy a Robin Hood type of image in Lebanon. They have significant presence in UNIFIL AO and are equipped with sophisticated weapons. Their presence in South Lebanon poses a challenge to UNIFIL peacekeepers.

Palestinian refugees pose yet another challenge in UNIFIL AO. Numbering nearly 500,000, they are housed in 12 camps three of which fall in UNIFIL AO. Living in sub-human conditions, without citizenship rights, many of them indulge in unlawful activities like smuggling, gun-running and frequently engage in hostile acts against Israel. Despite having been in Lebanon for over six decades, they are yet to be granted citizenship rights and continue to 'dream' of returning to their homeland one day, a very remote possibility.

The IDF are a very well-equipped modern force with one of the best intelligence capability and state-of-the-art surveillance system super imposed on the sophisticated technical fence along the Blue Line. Tactical commanders of IDF enjoy a high degree of operational freedom. Highly sensitive to violations and movements along the Blue Line, their reactions are swift and violent, sometimes even automated. Peacekeepers have to react very rapidly to contain the fall out of such exchanges.

All of above, as well as the history of numerous armed conflicts in the past six decades, makes peacekeeping in the area that much more complex. Despite its criticism, UNIFIL has managed to keep peace and contain conflicts in its AO to a large extent. Initiatives like commencing tripartite meetings, marking of the Blue Line and also attempts to find a mutually acceptable solution to very complex situations like Ghajar Village have minimised flagrant situations significantly.

UNIFIL AO is bounded by Blue Line in the South and Litani River to the North. The Blue Line was drawn on the map by UN cartographers in the year 2000 to confirm Israeli withdrawal from Lebanon. Though not marked on ground prior to 2007, it has come to be recognised as the unofficial border between Lebanon and Israel. The peculiar aspect is that though UNIFIL is mandated to maintain peace between Lebanon and Israel, it is located entirely within Lebanon. Blue Line violations, mostly inadvertent, by Lebanese farmers and graziers often become a source of tension between the two sides and have the potential to escalate into a full-blown conflict. Presence of the IDF technical fence close to but not on the Blue Line also creates confusion in minds of the Lebanese regarding the precise layout of the border. It was to avoid such confusion that post 2006 conflict, UNIFIL initiated the process of physically marking the Blue Line.

UNIFIL and Principles of Peacekeeping

While the basic principles of peacekeeping i.e. Consent, Impartiality and Use (or non-use) of force remain unchanged, their application varies depending upon the circumstances and the operating environment. Peacekeeping operations are deployed only after consent of the parties involved and ordinarily not meant to 'enforce' peace through use of force. Force may, however, be used at the tactical level under certain circumstances, if acting in self-defence and defence of the mandate, but that would be an exception rather than the rule. The Security Council has given certain peacekeeping operations robust mandates authorising them to use all necessary means to carry out the mandate.

As regards adhering to the three cardinal principles of peacekeeping, UNIFIL has some peculiarities. Take *Consent* for example. Both Israel and Lebanon are signatories to the UN resolutions pertaining to UNIFIL. This implies that at strategic level consent of Hezbollah too exists, they being part of the Lebanese establishment. At tactical level though, things are not always so. Many a time, UNIFIL freedom of movement is obstructed by Hezbollah members leading to stand-offs with risk of rapid escalation. Resolving such a situation needs maturity, tact, and flexibility on part of peacekeepers as well as LAF that is alongside. Going strictly as per rule book might have disastrous consequences on the field. Similarly, should UNIFIL want to visit or inspect any IDF facility, it may be denied on the pretext that UNIFIL AO does not extend into Israel.

The second principle, *Impartiality*, is the sine qua non to success of any peacekeeping mission. Peacekeepers must take great care to ensure that all their actions are not only fair and impartial but be seen as such by all stake holders. Being neutral will not suffice, one has to be impartial and understand the difference between the two. Frequently, UNIFIL has been accused of playing favourites on many occasions by both parties, obviously for their own reasons. Peacekeepers should be prepared to deal with such accusations, stand firm and prove their impartiality by calling a spade a spade even if one or both parties do not like it.

Use (or non-use) of force is perhaps the most challenging principle to understand and apply since diplomacy does not come naturally to the combat soldier who is otherwise trained to use maximum force to achieve given objectives. In UNIFIL's case, post UNSCR 1701, the challenges increased since use of force was authorised under conditions other than purely self-defence. On many occasions, mainly when freedom of movement of peacekeepers was hindered, contingents behaved differently depending on their operating ethos, training, and experience. Mission leadership, therefore, had to quickly take stock of the matter and intervene in consultation with the hierarchy on both sides. Presence of LAF officers alongside helped a great deal in diffusing many situations that otherwise might have escalated beyond control.

Contribution of UNIFIL to Sustainable Peace

On the question whether traditional peace operations have contributed to sustainable peace, opinions may be divided. In UNIFIL's case too, critics have lamented the inefficacy of the force in ushering lasting peace in the region. One must understand that such problems can only be resolved politically. A military force can at best contain such situations and prevent escalation which UNIFIL has done quite successfully most of the time. That it could not prevent the outbreak of hostilities in 2006 can be attributed to its weak mandate, inadequate resources including a much reduced strength, besides the fact that Hezbollah violated the spirit of the UN Resolution by committing a hostile act against Israel on Israeli territory, killing few IDF soldiers and kidnapping two.

Post the 2006 conflict, at UNIFIL's behest, a mechanism was put in place to hold monthly tripartite meetings between IDF, LAF and UNIFIL to resolve tactical issues, a process that thankfully continues till date. It is interesting to note that this is the only forum where Lebanese and Israelis interact directly, as the two sides do not have diplomatic ties. This measure alone has contributed significantly towards bringing down tensions between the two sides and sustains peace.

As mentioned earlier, after the 2006 conflict, UNIFIL initiated the process of marking the Blue Line. After initial hiccups, the process took off, slowly but surely, and it is believed that today over 80% of the border is physically demarcated and marked with prominent Blue coloured barrels, cast in concrete, at regular intervals along the Blue Line. This has resulted in reducing the number of Blue Line violations manifold, mainly by preventing inadvertent crossings by innocent Lebanese civilians and livestock. One could consider this a major step towards achieving sustainable peace.

No doubt peacekeeping costs money and that perhaps is the foremost concern of member states while deliberating upon mission deployment and continuance. UNIFIL's yearly budget is approximately 500 million USD. On the face of it, this may seem huge and wasteful but one ought to remember that cost of war is far greater. The 2006 conflict itself cost the international community over 15 billion USD, besides huge losses of life and property on both sides. Member states need to appreciate this and continue their budgetary support to the mission till such time a lasting political solution is reached. Despite resource constraints, one can safely state that UNIFIL has performed creditably to sustain peace in this otherwise volatile region.

Ultimately, a peace operation to be effective and successful depends upon several factors, out of which only a few may be in the operation's control. Effectiveness would mainly depend on the larger political context and the combined efforts and commitment of all stake holders to sustain peace. Unfortunately, the latter are seldom present in any mission area. Political solutions are seldom forthcoming, and missions are burdened with mandates that lack focus and clear priorities.

Peacekeeping is still one of the most effective tools available to the UN to maintain international peace and security. That is why, despite criticism, demand for peacekeeping missions is ever on the increase. No doubt improvements can and should continue to be made to make peacekeeping more effective and, to its credit, UN has continuously endeavoured to do so. The Brahimi Repot, Capstone Doctrine and a host of similar measures are adequate pointers in this regard. Renewed political commitment on the part of member states, and increased financial support, as also recommended in the Brahimi Report, are key factors for improving effectiveness of UN peacekeeping.

Conclusion

That many recommendations of these reports are yet to be implemented is a cause for concern. Nevertheless, peacekeeping continues to evolve to keep pace with contemporary challenges and hopefully will maintain the trend in future too. Member states, besides empowering peacekeeping missions with requisite mandate and resources, should also support these endeavours politically with minimum caveats to give operational freedom to mission leadership. Simultaneously, political, social, and economic initiatives must be undertaken to address the root cause of the conflict and alleviate sufferings of the masses. If and when that happens, the world will surely be a much safer and more peaceful place to live.

Epilogue

Major General AK Bardalai (Retd) (Moderator)

Introduction

The three principles are considered as the first factor for successful peace operations. The experience of past decades suggests that adherence to the principles of peacekeeping is gradually becoming more challenging than when the concept of principles was conceived. In the UN publication – *UN Peacekeeping Operations: Principles and Guidelines* of 2008 – these principles have been oversimplified.[1] The principles, which are intricately connected, have different meanings at different levels and their interpretation varies from conflict to conflict. The opinions of the policymakers at the UN HQs, that of the practitioners and the outside views of the academicians are at variance. Consequently, there is a gap in the conceptual thinking on the principles and how these are applied in the field. Variation in their understanding or interpretation finally results in mandate implementation.

Principles of Peacekeeping

Peacekeeping is an instrument designed to preserve the peace, however fragile, where fighting has halted, and to assist in implementing agreements achieved by the peacemakers. It was the brainchild of Lester Pearson, Canada's Minister of

---

1   *United Nations Peacekeeping Operations: Principles and guidelines* (New York: UN Department of Public Information, 2008).

External Affairs (later Prime Minister) and the UN Secretary-General, Dag Hammarskjold. It was a concept conceived as a diplomatic key to open the path for further negotiations for a peaceful resolution of the conflict. It, therefore, is part of the whole process of peace and tested for the first time in the First United Nations Emergency Force (UNEF I).[2] Over the years, peacekeeping has evolved primarily from the military model of observing cease-fires and the separation of forces after inter-state wars, to incorporate a complex model of many elements – military, police and civilian – working together to help lay the foundations for sustainable peace. The operations undertaken, based on this concept, are referred to as either a Peacekeeping Operation (PKO) or, at times, a peacekeeping mission. When Dag Hammarskjold identified the principles of peacekeeping after the deployment of UNEF in 1958, it was more in the context of inter-state conflict. Even non-P5 members could help to return peace and the use of force was limited to rare occasions.[3] However, with the number of parties to the conflict increasing in intra-state conflict and the violence becoming more intense, the current alignment of the peacekeeping operations seems to have changed the very definition of the principles.

The consent is no more absolute and availability of consent at the strategic, operational, and tactical level is rare. Consent is mostly conditional. Despite the comprehensive peace agreement, consent seems to be allusive. But that the consent is conditional is not a new trend. It was so earlier but has become more obvious now. When it is available, it is generally out of some motive which could be to buy time like

---

2   Indar Jit Rikhye, *The Theory & Practice of Peacekeeping* (New York: C Hurst & Company, 1984), 224-27.

3   Norrie MacQueen, *Peacekeeping and International System* (New York: Routledge, 2006),74–78; United Nations, *"Summary Study of the Experience Derived from the Establishment and Operation of the Force: Report of the Secretary-General, A/3943,"* (October 9, 1958).

despite the signing of the Arusha Agreement, the emergence of Hutu power in Rwanda in 1994, or Mohd Aideed agreeing to the deployment of 500 peacekeepers only for escort of a humanitarian convoy in 1993.[4] For that matter, even Hezbollah gave its approval for the current UNIFIL in return for not naming them in the UNSCR 1701. Even in the case of UNMISS, when the fight for the turf was always predictable once South Sudan became independent, the reason for the parties to sign the comprehensive peace agreement is the intriguing part. Hence, the principle of consent is always at the fence and ever ready to be recanted at the slightest pretext. When that happens, first there will be an obstruction to freedom of movement followed by increased hostility and attack on the peacekeepers.

Impartiality replaced the principle of neutrality when the non-P5 members could no longer contribute capable peacekeepers when the violence became intense. But the difference between neutrality and impartiality remained either confused or intentional because of the national interest of the respective TCCs. There are instances of peacekeepers not using force even for self-defence. What happened in the civilian camp in Malaka in South Sudan in February 2016 is an example that shows how difficult and precarious such situations may be.[5] When hundreds of SPLA soldiers stormed Terrain Hotel in South Sudan on 16 July 2016, beaten up and raped foreign worker and killed a journalist in broad daylight, and the peacekeepers did not respond for hours, the

---

4   Lise Morje Howard, *UN Peacekeeping in Civil Wars* (Cambridge: Cambridge University Press, 2008), 25–30.

5   The civilian camp, co-located with the UN base, housed more than 37,000 people mainly from Dinkar and Nuer communities. When the fighting broke out between these two groups, many civilians rushed towards to the UN base for shelter. Fearing a situation which could go out of control, the peacekeeping contingent failed to react.

UNMISS compromised impartiality and lost its credibility.[6] Force Intervention Brigade (FIB) is yet another example of the MONUSCO's losing status of impartiality. FIB, which was created in the wake of M 23 rebels taking over the town of Goma in 2012, was able to defeat M 23.[7] But it not only failed to neutralise other groups, it did also not even target 66 out of 70 armed groups. When FIB, which represents MONUSCO, operates along with FARDC in support of the corrupt Congolese government, which is responsible for 65 per cent HR violence, the credibility and legitimacy of the UN is lost.

Even in traditional peace operation like UNIFIL, which is deployed in Lebanon and NOT in both countries, Israelis forever complain UNIFIL taking the side of Lebanon. On the other hand, most in South Lebanon and Hezbollah are suspicious of the contingents of the western nations passing intelligence to Israel.[8] The centre of gravity of UNIFIL's credibility lies in the eyes of the local population of South Lebanon. Howard also quoted Major General Luciano Portolano, the former UNIFIL Force Commander stating that the relationship with the local population is the UNIFIL's operational centre of gravity.[9] Therefore, any attempt to do anything that is against the interest of Hezbollah is to

---

6   Lauren Spink and Matt Wells, "Under Fire: The July 2016 Violence in Juba and UN Response," *Center for Civilians in Conflict*, October 5, 2016, https://civiliansinconflict.org/publications/research/fire-july-2016-violence-juba-un-response.

7   Charles T. Hunt, "All Necessary Means to what Ends? The Unintended Consequences of the 'Robust Turn' in UN Peace Operations," *International Peacekeeping* 24, no.1 (2017): 111-13.

8   Vanessa Frances Newby, "Credibility through Aid," *Peacekeeping in South Lebanon: Credibility and Local Cooperation* (New York: Syracuse University Press, 2018), 158.

9   Lise Morje Howard, *Power in Peacekeeping* (New York: Cambridge University Press, 2019), 114.

annoy the local population and is crossing the red line and is perceived as partial. When the local population withdraws their support, even the Lebanese government will withdraw its support. But same Israel urges that the current deployment of UNDOF should revert to its original deployment i.e. both sides of the disengagement line. Because the current deployment is on Israel side, which took place after ISIS reached Syria, it only looks at the Israeli side and not the Syrian side.

Impartiality, to an extent, is a matter of perception which is formed by the history of the peacekeepers. For example, Belgium's impartial status, being the past colonial master of Rwanda, was doubted from the time 450 Belgian troops landed in Rwanda in November 1993. Most of the soldiers who had returned from Somalia were arrogant in their behaviour. Similarly, in Lebanon, the Italians, the French or the Indians are viewed differently both by the Lebanese Government as well as Hezbollah.

The use of force is by far is the most controversial of the three principles. More often than not, these principles have been interpreted differently by different TCCs, more specifically in the context of the use of force in self-defence. There are varying interpretations of the term self-defence. According to one of the former Secretaries-General of the UN, Mr Kurt Waldheim, self-defence includes "resistance to attempts by forceful means to prevent it from discharging its duties under the mandate of the Security Council".[10] Cox noted that force can be used in self-defence in a mission under Chapter VI. However, a reference to Chapter VII in some mission is absent. As a result, the same task creates confusion. Cox further observed that while some TCCs

---

10   UN Security Council, *Report of the Secretary General on the Implementation of Security Council Resolution 340 (1973)*, S/11052/Rev.1 (October 27, 1973).

interpret the tasks in the spirit of what Waldheim defined, a few TCCs use this confusion to shy away from using force even in self-defence. According to her, TCCs' reluctance to use force could be driven by domestic political considerations as well. Participating in peace operations when the host nation has consented is different from being part of a multinational force and use force even for the right reasons to impose the Security Council resolution. In this regard, she observed that, "It may be harder to get States to contribute troops to peacekeeping operations if they may be involved in the use of coercive force. This may be due to constitutional reasons".[11] But those who do not want to use it either because of fear of casualty or some other reasons will never use it even in Chapter VII. On the other hand, there are examples of peacekeepers not abdicating their moral responsibility of protecting the lives of innocent civilians no matter what the mandate is.

Therefore, peacekeeping principles are not absolute as these were thought to be and will continue to cloud our mind. The question, therefore, is how does one implement the mandate?

Mandate Implementation

In all references to the performance of peacekeeping missions, mandate becomes the first casualty. A stronger mandate supported by adequate resources and capable peacekeepers will certainly help to implement the mandate. However, if those who are entrusted with the responsibility to implement the mandate are not willing because of one reason or the other, no matter how strong is the mandate and how capable the peacekeepers are, the peacekeeping missions will not be able to implement the mandate. Given the tradition of 'Pen

---

11 Katherine E Cox, "Beyond Self-Defence: United Nations PKOs & and the Use of Force," *Denver Journal of International Law and Policy* 27 (1999), 271.

Holder' in mandate formulation is not likely to go away soon, the mandate will continue to remain as the product of the negotiation and adjustment amongst the P5 members.[12] The wording of the mandate can be stronger. But how to implement the mandate will remain silent. Further, the mandate will mention what to do but NOT what is not to be done. There will not be any reference to the red lines which if crossed, the mission can be jeopardised.

Conclusion

How to, therefore, implement the mandate when adherence to the principles of peacekeeping is a challenge? I believe that answer to this question lies firstly in the understanding of the challenges of the principle of peacekeeping and in the answer to the simple question – what a peacekeeper is expected to do? If the peacekeepers are primarily to save the lives of innocent human beings and protection of innocent lives have become the core objective of the peacekeeping operations, the commanders on the ground should formulate their mission objectives, no matter what or how is it worded in the Security Council resolution. This will not only help to maintain the status of impartiality but also bring credibility and legitimacy to the peace operation. There is no better example other than the instructions of the NORDBAT contingent (comprising reservists) commander to his platoon commanders on mandate implementation in Srebrenica in 1993. On being deployed, he reminded his platoon commanders that their mission objective is to save innocent lives. And to do that they can disobey all other orders. The contingent commanders did come under pressure but did not budge.[13] To be able to

---

12 UN Security Council Report, The Pen Holder System, *Research Report*, December 2018, https://www.securitycouncilreport.org/atf/cf/%7B65BFCF9B-6D27-4E9C-8CD3-CF6E4FF96FF9%7D/Penholders.pdf

13 Tony Ingesson, *The Politics of Combat: The Political and Strategic Impact of Tactical-level Subcultures, 1939–1995* (Lund: The Faculty of Social

set such a clear mission objective, it takes years of grooming on profession, integrity, and honesty.

Science and Department of Political Science, 2016): 231–282, http://lup.lub.lu.se/record/8871111; Tony Ingesson, "Trigger-happy, Autonomous, and Disobedient: Nordbat 2 and Mission Command in Bosnia," *The Strategy Bridge*, September 21, 2017, https://thestrategybridge.org/the-bridge/2017/9/20/trigger-happy-autonomous-and-disobedient-nordbat-2-and-mission-command-in-bosnia.

Major Takeaways

Major General SB Asthana, SM, VSM (Retd)

Trends in Peace Operations

The contours of global politics are changing and so are the nature of conflict and the nature of peace operations. The traditional peacekeeping was suited to keep peace in interstate conflict in last few decades but the frequency of interstate conflicts has been reducing and intrastate conflicts are on the rise. In traditional peacekeeping missions also, where peace operations were in vogue to keep peace in interstate conflict, there is an unavoidable change in the focus towards controlling the intrastate elements of conflict because of increasing violence. The fact that the peacekeeping is now being referred as peace operations, and the primacy of peace building efforts in peacekeeping operation is increasing, there is a need to revisit the principles and mandates for peace operations. Bulk of the peacekeeping missions today are stabilisation missions having the role to protect civilians (POC) inbuilt in the mandate. There are non-state actors who do not follow any rule of law and, therefore, peacekeepers get involved in protection of civilians as a fate accompli, even where POC is not part of the mandate. There is also a debate that counter insurgency operations should fall within the mandate of peace operations or otherwise?

Are the Peacekeeping Principles Relevant in Today's Peace Operations?

The principles of peacekeeping, namely 'Consent of Parties to the Conflict', 'Impartiality', and 'Non use of Force except in case of self-defence or defence of Mandate', were applicable to traditional peacekeeping. With involvement of a large number of non-state actors, the number of parties to the conflict has increased. Non-state actors remain outside the preview of consent or any law abiding preposition/agreement. With multifarious actors in operational environment, with some having conflicting interest, any action taken by peacekeepers in good faith may not suit some actor; hence, even if it is as per mandate, peacekeepers will be accused of partiality by that actor. It is difficult to maintain impartiality, in real sense, in such environment. South Sudan, Mali and many others are cases in point. Bulk of the missions today are the stabilisation missions involving POC, the need to disarm, demobilise and reintegrate (DDR), prevent human right (HR) violations and ensure socio economic recovery. The peacekeepers when confronted with non-state actors, which are heavily armed and ready to inflict casualties on civilians as well as themselves, find it necessary to use force for protection, in such circumstances which may/may not be covered under the mandate. Unfortunately, the United Nation charter is silent on use of force against non-state actors.

Issues Related to Use of Force

For missions requiring POC, the UNSC needs to ensure that there is robust mandate and requisite political support for use of force, based on the operating environment and the risk involved. The peacekeepers should follow peacekeeping principles of impartiality, minimum use of force adequate to tide over the crisis and the rules of engagement, to the extent possible, even in dealing with unforeseen situations. Under the circumstances where the life of people or peacekeepers is gravely threatened, they should be prepared, trained and equipped to use force to protect civilians as well as themselves. Recommendations of the Santos Cruz Report[1] on security of peacekeepers need implementation by all concerned. In situations like South Sudan which is new country, it was seen that the state did not have requisite capacity to protect its population and there was also suspicion of state support to some groups who were causing casualties. Under such circumstances, a balance between state and humanitarian needs must be made by the peacekeepers.

A practical problem which is often felt by peacekeepers while using force for POC is lack of actionable intelligence in dealing with non-state actors. Acquiring intelligence in peacekeeping missions becomes a challenge due to issues of neutrality, impartiality and privacy of host country. United Nations, therefore, needs to have a clear policy for making actionable intelligence necessary for POC to peacekeepers through all the latest means available. It is, therefore, necessary that the peacekeepers must be equipped with necessary wherewithal for gathering intelligence in terms of technology, equipment and well considered policies.

It is also seen that there has been hesitancy in use of force by certain contingents due to fear of human rights activists, media and allegations for criminal act, which sometimes leads to complacency. It is, however, seen that most actions taken by peacekeepers in good faith have been commended, and, therefore, the apprehension of hiding behind the

---

1   Cruz Santos (2017), Improving Security of United Nations Peacekeepers: We need to change the way we are doing business, UN Website, Accessed on February 25, 2021. https://peacekeeping.un.org/sites/default/files/ improving_security_of_united_nations_peacekeepers_report.pdf

mandate and not protecting civilians is misplaced and has been criticised, wherever it has occurred.

Deployment of UN Peacekeepers to deal with Terrorism

It is understandable that counter insurgency operation is not the role of peacekeepers, but when confronted with armed non state actors equipped with modern weaponry, ready to cause casualties, then peacekeepers have to undertake such role for their own safety and POC. It is, therefore, necessary that all contingents going for stabilisation mission should be attuned, trained, equipped and mentally prepared to take on counterinsurgency operations, even if not mandated, because any failure by peacekeepers in confrontation with non-state actors shows professionalism of that contingent, country and UN in poor light. However, no matter how well trained and well equipped peacekeepers are, when it comes to defend either themselves or the civilians against the terrorist attacks, the three principles of peacekeeping will be the first casualty.

Closing Remarks

Dr TCA Raghavan

At the outset, I would like to say how very delighted I am on behalf of the ICWA that this planned series of discussions on UN peacekeeping has begun with such an excellent and thought-provoking session. The interventions of Lieutenant General Nambiar, Ambassador Mukerji and Dr Cedric provided a larger overview that was very thought-provoking and set the stage for the subsequent interventions by Lieutenant General Chander Prakash, Lieutenant General Singha, Lieutenant General Nehra and, finally, the wrapping up by Major General Asthana.

The mix of individual experiences and reflections on those experiences within the larger challenges of UN peacekeeping provides some insight into the issues which confront UN peacekeeping today. We heard a whole range of the issues that are involved, beginning with the distinction — it's not a water tight distinction but nevertheless, for analytical purposes that distinction is very important – between traditional peacekeeping operations and the non-traditional ones. This distinction on the ground often does not exist and I think General Nehra had spoken about while there may be a strategic consensus, which underpins a particular traditional peacekeeping operation, nevertheless on the ground that strategic consensus does not prevent numerous other frictions and tensions from playing a larger than life role.

Personally, I found the discussion today fascinating because it told us about the location of professional soldiers in a diplomatic environment. One question which has always interested me is the divergence between the diplomatic approach or way of thinking and the way a trained military mind thinks. Diplomats are trained to evaluate and understand intentions, gauge interests; the military mind is trained to evaluate capacities. This distinction of course is well known but when a professional soldier is placed in a diplomatic context, it throws up a very rich array of reflections and impressions. I think in the context of UN peacekeeping and the challenges it faces, today's discussion was very enriching and I must say that it sets the stage very well for the subsequent events that will follow.

Very thought-provoking issues were also raised by General Nambiar and Ambassador Asoke Mukerji; firstly, terrorism and counter-terrorism in the context of UN peacekeeping; secondly, the dynamic of peacekeeping versus peace building. Possibly this is something which we can reflect upon in subsequent sessions and possibly explore further.

Most of all, I would like to thank the USI and Major General BK Sharma for having worked with us in first visualising and then planning out this series of webinars. I look forward to the subsequent discussions.